Married in Paris— A Memoir

Married in Paris—
A Memoir

A Young Woman's Plight in
the city of light against Military
Might overcoming her Fright
and gaining Insight

PAT ENDERLE

Copyright © 2003 by Pat Enderle.

Library of Congress Number: 2003096356
ISBN: Hardcover 1-4134-2931-9
Softcover 1-4134-2930-0

All rights reserved. No part of this book may be reproduced or transmitted in any form or by any means, electronic or mechanical, including photocopying, recording, or by any information storage and retrieval system, without permission in writing from the copyright owner.

This book was printed in the United States of America.

To order additional copies of this book, contact:
Xlibris Corporation
1-888-795-4274
www.Xlibris.com
Orders@Xlibris.com

Contents

ACKNOWLEDGMENTS 9

INTRODUCTION 11

HOW DID I GET HERE? 12

FEARS MELT 21

SETTLING IN 30

DOING THE TASKS 39

SHOCKED BY EMBASSY,
SHOCKED BY ELECTRICITY 65

THE EVIL WOMAN 72

THE CONCIERGE 80

L'OREAL 84

MARRIED IN BOULOGNE-BILLANCOURT 88

THE HONEYMOON 97

Dedication

To my daughter, Nicole,

for her faith and encouragement.

Acknowledgments

These stories were told many times around a dinner table so I have to thank Betty Spears for her simple suggestion, "You should write a book." My thanks also to Betty's daughter, Jennifer Darling, who works in publishing and gave me encouragement. Once some words were on the page, many friends inspired and reassured my efforts.

I am grateful:

To Lynne Duesenberg, who found my stories exciting.

To Katie Luellen, who helped me explain things for the younger generation.

To Frances Reisbeck, Lin Amey, and Ginny Bank who gave the book a read and gave me useful feedback.

Introduction

I have attempted to write a memoir of my adventures when I decided to get married in Paris. The events began with feelings of trepidation, but at the conclusion I gained confidence. I wandered headfirst into perplexity and encountered obstacles that, when transcended, modified my worldview and gave me strength of commitment. Implicating the French for all the difficulties I encountered is not an impartial assessment, as the United States Army played a leading role in my troubles. My ignorance and innocence flavored each experience, but my youth was an asset I did not recognize until age and responsibility changed my perspective.

How did I get here?

I left the United States Saturday, September 7, 1963. I have flown so far and for so long it is now Sunday, September 8. Low clouds cover Paris as we approach Orly Airport. My forehead is attached to the window as the plane sinks lower and lower back to earth. I catch glimpses of the ground through the clouds. Gazing on the twisting roads and hedge rows of the French countryside and peering into thick woods fascinates me. Such a contrast between this and the Jeffersonian homesteading of the non-timbered American mid-west landscape scarred with straight, parallel section lines of roads and fencing that I have just left behind.

Saturday morning, September 7, dawned with me safely curled in bed hidden under my covers. My sister approached, flung the covers away and declared, "Time to get up, you have far to go today." I flew after my covers, grasped them with tight fists, and returned to my hiding place. "I'm not going," I say. "You have to go," she gasps. "You have it all arranged."

I spent months making plans and preparations. But on the morning, when I must begin to advance my scheme, I only wanted the safety of my familiar bed. I could not embark on an adventure full of unknowns. I was about to leave the United States. I have never been out of the country. I am going to get married.

MARRIED IN PARIS—A MEMOIR

I have never been married. I will be taking an airplane. I have never flown. I am leaving home. I am only nineteen, or am I a full-grown nineteen? Which is it? I was very scared.

I have good reason to be scared. We deplane from the rear of the aircraft. As I descend the steep stairs, the cool morning air tries to massage my face into alert condition. It is just the first of September, but already the United States Army troops stationed in Paris have changed to their winter uniforms because the cold weather chills the forces. I was born and raised in Colorado but just as with heat, there is a difference between dry cold and wet cold. The Paris winter temperature hovers just about at freezing, but this damp cold penetrates deep inside my body. Eventually I learn to use leather and wool, boots and scarves to stave off the shivers. I didn't know it then, but Paris will keep her overcast skies, and it will be ten months before I see the stars, the moon, or a bright sun again.

I follow my fellow passengers across the tarmac to the open door. As I enter, the only way to go is up the stairs. A uniformed woman working for the airline standing inside the doorway says something, which strikes terror in my heart. It is not what she said, but the frightening way she said it. She spoke to me in French! My face screams panic as I look at her and with all the savoir-faire of Jethro Bodine. I say, "huh?" She repeats in English, "Proceed up the stairs and to your left." A long hall leads me to the crowd jostling to pass through the passport check. I await my turn without looking up, for fear I will see Al and the excitement will overpower me.

My fiancé, Al, is six months older than me but still just nineteen. At such an advanced age, we surely have all the wisdom of life. He has pledged his life to the United States Army. The army requested he serve his country in France. Now, I let my heart or my youth or my insanity pull me in his path.

When Al graduated from high school the year before me, he worked in a candy factory and a gas station. Neither of which would lead to a career. He talked to the representatives of "Uncle Sam" and found them more than willing to find him a career. He went away for basic training, leaving me alone and lonely. I wrote him every day. The army kept him busy. He did not write often, but when he wrote he kindly returned my letters with corrections to my spelling, grammar, and punctuation. His early years in Catholic school and my early years in public school, with what must have been a slight case of dyslexia, became evident when written communication connected our lives. This may sound cruel and unromantic, but I think assisting your loved one in conquering a defect is the essence of benevolence.

Finally, I submit my passport for inspection. It receives a hearty stamp, and I move through the checkpoint. I look all around for welcoming arms. I find none. It crosses my mind that there may be some sort of mix-up. Did Al think it was another day or time? I don't want to panic. I have traveled this far; maybe I can manage my own way. I look to the signage to instruct me the way to my luggage. I see an abundance of signs, but the information I cannot comprehend. What is going on here? Everything is written in French. No problem, I will simply follow my fellow travelers again. I study faces to pair them from the ones from my flight. No good; all my folks have vanished. Right then, I know what I shall do next. I will find a place to sit . . . and cry. I turn completely around. Every seat is occupied. Crying, while I stand with a hatbox about to spill its contents into bustling foot traffic, is not appealing.

I carry a cardboard hatbox in an attempt to save money. Overseas flights require baggage weight to be under specified poundage or else you pay a hefty fine for the excess. I had expected to pay around fifty dollars for suitcase tonnage, so I happily complied with the forty-dollar charge.

Setting up a household, which is what I plan to do in Paris, requires an abundance of objects, gadgets, and commodities. I mailed a four-piece set of dishes and flat ware, Tupperware, and linens to enhance our living arrangements. The large, heavy purse hanging over my shoulder contains make-up, lotion, shampoo; any compact but weighty item. The cardboard hatbox dripping from my forearm is collapsing, as am I. It is filled to the top with shoes and a tin of chocolate chip cookies baked by Al's mom that morning so Al could receive them fresh.

Will he receive them fresh? Will he receive them at all? Have I missed a letter from him about where to meet? Have all my letters reached him about when and where I'll be arriving? I left his phone number back in the States, so I can't call him. As panic seeps from every pore, my life with Al begins to rush through my mind.

We met in high school. New in town, he and his brothers had found their way into my sister's crowd. He knew me, but didn't think much of me; and I knew him, but never considered dating my little sister's friends. One fall Friday, my sister told him I liked him, would he be my date with the gang that night. She told me he liked me, and wanted me to be his date. With nothing better to do, we took pity on each other. I don't remember where we went or what we did; I only remember that he kissed me. As when Prince Charming kissed Snow White, my head and heart never turned to another after that kiss. The year was 1959.

The spring of 1962 he went to basic training in Missouri for three months. Anywhere outside our home state of Colorado felt like a long way away to me. After basic training, he returned home by bus. I picked him up at the bus station. I wanted to run up to him and throw my arms around him and feel the warmth of a long embrace. This didn't happen. I know him well enough that I was not surprised he didn't want to kiss in front of his buddies. But I still felt disappointed. As far as suitors go, he was liberal and passionate in private, but conservative and prudent in public.

We had two brief but wonderful weeks together before he wentto New Jersey for communication maintenance training. He will be attending this school for six months; half a year. I thought a year was a lifetime, and that New Jersey must be as far away as he could get. At the end of his school he received his orders for his next assignment. He was sent to France. France! That was very far away. France! I couldn't even drive there if I had a good car. How would I survive?

He was given one-month leave and enough money to take a bus from his post on one side of New Jersey to the post on the other side of New Jersey from where he would board a ship to travel to France.

With the meager amount of money we had between us, he purchased a one-way plane ticket from New Jersey to Colorado. The month of leave he had before his departure to France included both Christmas and New Year's. I could not comprehend his being anywhere but home. His brothers went with me to pick him up at the airport. Again, no smooching.

We had a lovely Christmas. I thought the timing perfect for him to give me an engagement ring. That made sense in my young, fanciful mind; but really, if he had money for an engagement ring, he could have bought a roundtrip plane ticket. We had a nice New Year's. His mother liked having her first-born home for the holidays. No one wanted to think about his leaving, or of how he would return to New Jersey.

Military people have a privilege called a "hop." You go to a military base and "hop" a plane, going where you want to go. We spent a day trying to make this kind of arrangement. There were no planes going to New Jersey. Backed into a corner, we had to break down and tell his parents that we had no money and no way for him to get back to New Jersey. This ended our happy holidays in more ways than one. His Dad's Christmas bonus bought Al a ticket to New Jersey. The rest of his family, hoping for booty from Dad's bonus, waved goodbye to Al with mixed feelings.

In the six months Al was going to army school in New Jersey, I had graduated from high school and attended school to become a hairdresser. Al left for France in January, and I started working in April as a hairdresser at a local solon. At that time, 1963, people still traveled to Europe by ocean liner. I began to look into the possibility of becoming a hairdresser on an ocean liner and getting close enough to France to pay him a visit. I wrote to Al to tell him about my ocean liner idea. He wrote back: "If you get over here for a visit I want you to stay and marry me."

My heart flipped. Why not? I will just go there and we will get married. It sounded so easy. This was not the first time he had proposed. As a sophomore I could not go to the Junior-Senior prom unless asked by a Junior or Senior. One day I was hinting for Al to invite me to the prom. They must have been pretty strong hints, because he asked me to marry him. Wow, what does a girl say to that? If I say, "No thank you, I'm not thinking of marriage right now," he might not bother to ask me to the prom. On the other hand, if I become his betrothed, he will have to take me to the prom. We did go to the prom together that year, and the next. So three years after the proposal in person, the follow-up by mail changed a general proposal into one with a more finite timeframe.

After my heart flipped, my mind started flapping. I really had no idea what lay ahead. I had never been away from home. I had never been on an airplane. I had never been married. I had never been out of the country.

My father's younger brother graduated from high school in 1944, a week after my birth. He immediately joined the army. War still raging in Europe and the Pacific, my uncle's deployment almost twenty years before Al's departure called for the same destination, France. My uncle now rests among a wide field of white crosses and six-corner stars in Luxembourg. He did not fall by enemy fire; rather, diphtheria reached out and ended his fight and fighting. This tragedy menaced our family.

Mindful of this heartbreak, I told my doctor of my travel plan. He said there were no health requirements for going to France, but he thought it would be a good idea for me to get the typhoid series. My records show I received diphtheria shots as a child. Typhoid inoculations are given in a series of three, then followed with annual boosters. Typhoid must be a retched disease because the shots are miserable. The first shot made me so sick I spent a day on the couch doing nothing but considering not having any more shots and not going to France. The other two, and the booster I received a year later, all made me feel as if I had the flu.

I wrote Al and told him I was coming to France to marry him. The complications of communicating by overseas mail breaks down as my letters fly east, and his letters fly west, passing each other in flight. It takes over a week for mail to go each direction, so it can be almost a month before one of us answers a question asked by the other.

When I read Al's letter lamenting the cost of living in Paris and suggesting we might want to hold off any immediate plans, I felt as if he was asking me to jump off a speeding locomotive. Didn't he just write and say he wanted me to come over and marry him?

I was staying with a friend while her parents were gone when I received the "marry me" letter. I spent an entire day in bed, in her house, as she went to work, came back for lunch, returned to work, and returned home after work.

She was concerned about my mental health because I was not physically ill. It had taken me all that time to decide to get married. Now, Al was saying, wait.

I had already begun the process of attaining a passport, purchasing a wedding dress, and getting airline tickets.

The wedding dress I bought was beautiful. Its length is just below my knees. It has a hip-length over-skirt which hooks with a small bow in front. The sleeves are three-quarter length, and it has a straight neck. It is just plain white, shiny material, no lace. My veil is shoulder-length plain net attached to a pillbox hat.

The summer of 1963, TWA offered a new service never before possible – non-stop flights from Denver to Paris. These flights were only available on Tuesdays, Thursdays, and Saturdays. Perfect. I picked Saturday. As best as I can recall, the ticket cost three hundred dollars. Two weeks before my departure date, the airline called to inform me they no longer offered Saturday departure. All my plans surround this date. Thursday before, was too early; I was not ready yet. Tuesday after, my mind could not comprehend. I had a very structured life up to, and including Saturday morning, September 7, 1963. When I try to imagine the future past that date, it is like looking into a clouded pool. There must be something there, but nothing was visible. I reluctantly accepted their offer of a flight from Denver to New York, then New York to Paris, on Saturday. This could be trouble.

My family celebrated birthdays, like many families. The birthday child picked the place for dining out. One year my younger sister selected the Sky Chef Restaurant at Denver's Stapleton Airport. That dinner brought me as close to an airplane as I had ever been. I did not know if I had fear of flying, but if that were to develop on the first leg of a flight with a lay-over, it would be possible for me to high tail it back to Colorado on a train. Leaving Al and the City of Lights, awaiting my arrival.

Now he was asking me to put all my plans on hold, for what? For how long? I decided to telephone him to clarify whether go or no go.

Telephoning tore at my pocketbook. A call costing five dollars a minute could easily amount to a substantial sum. This connection also had to be placed by an overseas operator. I phoned in the late afternoon, not considering the time difference. The number I had belonged to a common phone used by all the soldiers working in the area. I placed the call person-to-person. I waited the longest hour of my life for the operator to reach me and inform me my party was on the line.

The call caught Al getting off work at midnight and loading his few possessions into a friend's car for a ride to his newly leased hotel room. After seven months he could finally afford to move out of the cramped army facility where eight guys, all working different shifts, sleep in one room. This dark room contained sleeping soldiers twenty-four hours a day. These men maintained a communication center, with non-stop activity. The army housed eight of the communication center's newest non-commissioned soldiers until they were able to get on their feet financially and find accommodations locally.

I told him about the arrangements consuming my life. I presented one simple question: Do you want me to come over there and marry you or not? His reply had only one request. "Okay," he said. "Come on over but bring lots of money."

As I prepared for my embarkation, I realized the phone bill would arrive after my departure. I left thirty-five dollars to cover the cost, and hoped it would not be more. In time, ten dollars was returned to me. Al and I had managed to make wedding plans and travel plans in five minutes. Maybe, plan was too strong a word. If you suddenly plan to jump off a cliff, have you really, as the dictionary states, made a diagram showing the arrangement of jumping off a cliff? The dictionary goes on to say a plan is to devise a scheme for doing. Flying to France and getting married did not include all the preparations our scheme for doing would need. Whether out of love, out of loneliness, or out of suddenly being pressed for a response, his reply, "Okay, come on over but bring lots of money" was more a plea than a plan.

In the days of bouffant hairstyles, many women had weekly, standing appointments with their hairdresser. My regular customers gave attention to the development of my adventure as it advanced with each of their visits. I don't remember any advice of caution from these women, ranging in age from twenty-five to sixty-five. I guess since I had reached the age of great wisdom my ears were not accustomed to receiving information that would lead me away from my goal. Years later, I asked my mother about her thoughts, as I made ready to depart. "I told you not to go," was her emphatic reply. I admit, I have no memory of that.

I sold my car. Friends and family were very lavish with going-away gifts. My customers all tipped generously the last week I worked. I was accumulating what seemed like a tidy sum of money, but would it be enough? How much would be enough?

Al talked to the clerk in his commander's office to see what he needed to get married. The army, as always, had applications and regulations, and according to The Status of Forces Agreement, the agreement General Eisenhower signed with the French government at the end of World War II, the French government, conforming to their laws, handles all civil legal matters for the American military and their families. The army and the French both required anyone under the age of twenty-one to have notarized parental permission to marry.

By noon of September 7, 1963 I had managed to remove myself from my bed and keep my appointment to have my hair done. In the weeks preceding this day, I had attained a passport, bought a one-way plane ticket, purchased a wedding dress, mailed boxes, packed my bags, and put all my affairs in order.

I am carrying notarized permission to marry from Al's parents and my mother. I also have a notarized copy of my father's death certificate. Am I ready for all the challenges that lie ahead? All the challenges? Including standing alone in the middle of Orly Airport dead-tired, a heavy bag on my shoulder, and a painful hatbox on my arm, unable to read the signs and nowhere to sit. I begin to tremble.

Fears Melt

I see Al hurrying toward me. All my fears melt like darkness at sunrise. Remembering our previous non-embracing convergence, I hand him the hatbox and say, "Hold this." I make no move to give him a kiss. It has been eight months since we have seen each other. He feels the no-kissing let down. He tells me later it is okay to kiss in Paris; everyone does.

He apologizes for his tardy arrival and introduces me to Sgt. Blessim. A car is a rare commodity for soldiers in Paris. Sgt. Blessim has graciously volunteered himself and his car to fetch me.

We locate baggage claim. I find my cases and place them on the customs counter. They are locked. The French customs personnel watch as I dance around with my hands on my face saying, "Oh my God, the keys."

Panic strikes; I have no memory of the keys after locking the cases a lifetime ago on the other side of the world. My weary mind moves back to cover the events of the day that changed my life forever.

My chauffeurs for the day were Al's parents. His mom picked me up for my appointment at the hairdresser. Then she drove me back home to get dressed. She gave me an orchid corsage and we loaded my bags. Then we picked up Al's dad and drove to the airport.

I completed the weigh-in and check-in of the matching two-piece luggage set. Al's mom bought the luggage set for me. The three of us located the departure door. The pleasant afternoon sun warmed our faces as we strolled out the door for the thirty or so feet from the door to the eight-foot chain-link fence. At that point, only ticketed passengers were allowed to cross the tarmac, approach the plane, and mount the steps. I leaned back against the fence post and looked at the planes and people. After a few minutes Al's mom asked, "Aren't you going to get on?"

The day before, I had lunch with my mother, just the two of us sharing our love in a long good-bye. She kept a brave face as she let her little bird go far from the nest. If she had been at the fence right then and said, "Don't go," I would not have gotten on that plane. But, Al's mom had already suffered an empty place in her nest, and she wanted me to go to be with him.

I turned to Al's mom and managed an "uh-uh" and began my trek to the plane. How could that walk be so long and so short at the same time? The large, heavy purse hung over my shoulder. The hatbox strung over my forearm, and the pretense of it being light as a feather was cutting deep into my skin. My acting ability and the cardboard's stability were both failing as I reached the top step.

The tiny step I took through the threshold of the plane represented the immense step I took through the threshold of my life. I was forever altered. But my suit held up well. I purchased a brown knit suit with an elastic waist for my travel ensemble. Its comfort and shape sustained to the end. The corsage and I both wilted.

Subsidized air travel relieved the airlines of the need to fill all seats. The plane was only one-third full. I listened to the safety instructions like an astronaut listening to the countdown. As the plane rumbled faster and faster down the runway, I wrapped my feet around the hatbox under the seat in front of me and pushed my ankle hard against my large purse. I didn't want my things to slide back as the plane took to the air. I had watched planes take off, and it appeared to me that they ascended at such an angle that everything not held in place would slide to the back of the plane.

I occupied the seat next to the window. An unfortunate businessman occupied the seat on the aisle. He must have planned an easy Saturday afternoon flight to New York and now, he found his reading interrupted as he stands to allow my trudging to and from the bathroom. My bladder had collected my panic and struggled to be at ease.

I am fascinated with my bird's eye view of the earth as it passes below. This sight keeps me enthralled until we land.

In New York I asked directions about every fifty feet. When I couldn't find an airport information desk, I asked directions from guys wearing army uniforms. It made no sense, but I already felt myself as part of the army community. When I saw no uniforms, army or airport personnel, I asked directions from anyone who looked nice. There were a lot of people in the airport, and except for me, everyone looked as if they knew where they were going. I really did feel like the disoriented hayseed depicted in movies. I found the area where I was to wait before boarding the Paris flight. I don't remember waiting long. I don't remember being scared. I had begun to feel excited.

Settled again in a window seat, my keen ear heard the same safety instructions. A glance at my fellow travelers revealed that not all of them were committing this vital information to memory. *The Jane Froman Story*, a film about a movie star and a trans-Atlantic plane crash, was one of my favorites as a child. The safety instructions and this movie memory merged in my head and added an additional layer of terror. The plane began to taxi. We maintained this mode of conveyance for so long that I thought we were driving to France. Then I heard an announcement that we had to return to the terminal to acquire a bag of mail. The plane turned and ambled back to the terminal. A short stop, the plane made another turn and then taxied again. In the time it took to taxi out and back and out again, the bright afternoon sun put on a spectacular setting performance, and blackness covered the vista seen from my window. The view was now speckled with stars and city lights.

The distractions of eating dinner and watching a movie checked time and fear. A mutely lit quiet time after the movie suddenly interrupted by bright lights and breakfast was designed to give the weary traveler a cheery response to the new day. It was a nice idea, but my foggy brain and rumbling intestines would not yield to the trick. I don't think I slept. I probably didn't because I had to keep up those numerous trips to the bathroom.

Customs grew tired of my digging through the big bag and dismissed me without inspection. Later I find the keys in the bottom of the big bag, such a small item among all the hefty stuff.

My first views of Paris are somewhat eschew as three adults, two large suitcases, my big purse, and the hatbox are all crammed into the smallest car I have ever seen. The car, a 1962 MG Midget, has only two seats so I perch on Al's lap and curl my head down until I fit under the roof. I catch quick peeks as the car speeds through the maze of Paris streets.

The size of the car quickly fades from mind when I see the size of the hotel room. Two adults, two large suite cases, a big purse, and a hatbox fill this space as well.

The hotel named the Georges is close to the Etoile, on a very small street off of Avenue Wagram. Al's room is on the fourth floor. We climb five flights of stairs. Starting from the ground floor, the first flight's climb takes us to floor one.

We walk the stairs because Al doesn't trust the elevator. For the first time in my life I inspect the guts of an elevator. It is one of those open elevators – a cage through which the elevator rises and falls –. It groans and moans, creaks and crawls; it is slower than walking up the stairs. The stairs circle around the open shaft so all the elevator parts are visible. I agree, Al has good reason to feel the stairs are the best choice.

I am introduced to the water closet half a flight from our room. Closet really is the optimum name for this type of bathroom; a small closet containing only a toilet. At the door of the room I see hanging on the wall, a sink. And what is that knee-high porcelain fixture next to the sink? It looks a lot like a toilet. A toilet next to the window? A toilet open to the room! But we just saw the toilet. Stunned, I just stare at the thing. I won't move into the room. Al and the hotel guy carrying bags are trying to get past me to lay down their loads. After the guy leaves I say to Al, "What is that?" "The bidet," he replies. *Oh ya, I have heard of this.* The things he finds ordinary after only a few months tell a tale of how far I have yet to go before my metamorphosis is complete.

The room contains a wardrobe, a small table, a chair and a bed. Only one person can walk around at a time because there is no room to pass. No closet, no TV, no radio, no telephone; a sleeping and reading room that's all. We occupy this room for only one week, but the boredom I stack up can fill a larger container of time. Al must work all day. In the morning we walk the six blocks to the army snack bar/cafeteria for breakfast. Then back to the hotel. Then Al goes to work. He comes to get me for lunch at the same snack bar. For romantic dining in the City of Lights, our pocketbook directs that we eat at this same military establishment. After a few days, we walk from the snack bar to Al's work, and he lets me go back to the hotel alone. Writing this with the perfect view allowed by hindsight; this behavior seems over protective. Putting on that young skin again, I really am a little lost soul with only a fragment of knowledge of the ways of the world.

We eat three times a day at the snack bar. Al might have skipped a meal to enjoy his mother's cookies, but I want my three squares because I do not like chocolate, and I need time out of that room. After our first couple of trips walking up and down the Champs Elysees for our grub,

I am ready to return home. It is nice being with Al, but this place is strange.

Taking all our meals at the snack bar gives me a chance to meet everyone with whom Al works plus their girlfriends (French, Swedish, and American) and other expatriates that make up our little community. This collection is anxious to meet me – the girl that came over from the States. I am highly complimented by a GI at a party one evening. He has imbibed to excess and says to me, "You know, all these guys have a girlfriend in the States who is coming over, but you are the only one that really did it."

The number-one question asked about happenings back home in the US of A is: "What are the popular songs?" I couldn't give a good answer. I hadn't thought about it before I left. If I had I could have picked up a Top Forty list. This wouldn't have been a good list anyway since back then most music got popular on either coast first, before it reached Colorado and the rest of Middle America. Beatlemania took over in the States during our absence, and we knew nothing about it. The French teens were involved with the British boys. But our collected fellowship did not trust the French teens to know what was cool. Apparently, the French kids did know and we were all in for a big surprise when we returned stateside. Elvis will always be the king, but new guys are now on top.

Two evenings of that first week, another friend with a car took us to meet the rental agent and scrutinize obtainable apartments. We see only one the first night. The agent thinks it is the best for us because it is on the direct metro line to Al's work (line six). We reject it because of the price and location. We want to be closer to the army bus route, and we must pay the agent one month's rent for rent, one month's rent for deposit, and one month's rent for her fee. The second night, she has a better lock on our interest. We look at two places.

The first place, I suffer embarrassment from which I think I will not recover. It has a three-quarter bed, small for two people. The rental agent, Al, and the apartment owner have a discussion in two languages, the agent translating back and forth about the small bed and if it can it be exchanged for a larger one. The driver-friend and I stand back. They might as well have been talking about my sex life in graphic detail, because that is what it feels like to me.

We select the second apartment a few blocks from Metro Porte De St-Cloud and the same distance from the army bus line. Al's metro ride to work takes about half an hour. We think this the best location for getting around, but we no longer reside in Paris. The couple of blocks distance from the metro puts us in an area called Boulogne-Billancourt. No line of demarcation separates us, but it makes a difference to the post office, the issuance of parking tickets, and all other government offices with which we deal. A childhood friend read my address, 9 rue Edouard Detaille, in the hometown paper and sent me a letter using this address and the city of Paris, where everyone thinks I live. Where I think I am. But the letter is returned undeliverable because my address is Boulogne-Billancourt, not Paris. It would have been such fun to have received that letter at my home. I am sorry I missed it. I only know of it because my sister told me about it.

I mention parking tickets because everyone with a car gets parking tickets – Parisians and GIs alike. The Paris traffic bureaucracy tracks unpaid parking tickets at an inert pace. Most GIs return to the States long before their commanding officer inherits the delinquent tolls. The Boulogne-Billancourt traffic officials on the other hand have a quicker response to overdue parking tickets. This is not a concern now, but as the months go by and our financial status and lifestyle change, this makes a difference.

It is standard practice to double or triple park at the wide end of the street where the street joins the boulevard. When Al would get home after midnight while working the evening shift, he had no choice but to park this way, as others did; he sometimes got a ticket. General knowledge among the GIs is to ignore parking tickets. A soldier in country three years or less can get dozens of parking tickets in Paris and be back in the States before he is tracked down. The commanding officer has to handle these tickets, and I don't know if they are dropped because the offending party is not available or if the army makes some kind of deal to pay them. Every once in a while a GI will extend his tour in Paris for one reason or another, and the tickets will catch up with him.

I think Al has less than ten tickets when his commanding officer calls to say that the city of Boulogne-Billancourt wants to take action on his tickets. Al said he would take care of them. After the call ends the officer calls right back and asks when Al is scheduled to rotate. Al replies, "Next week." The officer says, "Never mind," and hangs up. Since Al has such a short time before he leaves, the officer took whatever action was needed. We did not pay the tickets.

On these apartment-hunting trips I lived through my first traffic circles while seated where I can see the road. I could not see the road on the trip from the airport because of the way I was stuffed into the car. I had thought the rapid acceleration and slamming on of brakes through a Paris traffic circle with a French taxi driver scary beyond belief, until years later I experienced this terror in a Roman traffic circle with an Italian taxi driver.

Nights in the hotel room, I learn lessons of big-city life. Suffering from jet lag the first couple of days, I sleep whenever I want. This causes me to be awake at night while Al sleeps. I listen to the sounds from the sidewalk. The Paris shoe fashion is a pump with a short-pointed steel-tipped heel. These shoes make a pleasant *click, click, click* as they transport their wearer down the sidewalk. Price is the reason we occupied the fourth floor. The lower floors rent by the hour and have exotic décor with lots of mirrors. I hear the working women who rent these rooms as they come and go *click, click, click* up and down the sidewalk.

I arrive in Paris wearing white, Ked-like tennis shoes. This style shoe tracked me through all my high school years, but tennis shoes were never the style in Paris. I covet the steel-heeled pumps and spend hours window-shopping and doing the math converting francs to dollars in my head until we have the money to buy them. Once I am shoed in this fashion, and we purchase a long coat for me, not a jacket, my transformation is inaugurated. When I add a fake fur collar and an elegant umbrella, I begin to blend in. When Al's mother sees a picture of me dressed in these items, she comments that I have turned French.

The popularity of the steel-heeled pumps is so great that the Louvre requires women to remove their shoes and wear paper booties, to save the parquet floors from damage.

Settling In

We enter our new apartment building through a big door off a narrow sidewalk. Just inside on the left is the concierge apartment; on the right, another apartment. At the opposite end of the short, wide entry hall are two more apartments, one on either side. The elevator is on the right just before the back apartment door. The elevator is large enough to hold three, maybe four, people. The stairs are at the very back of the building. The stairs go up half a floor to a landing then turn the other direction to the first floor, turn to the next landing, and so on. Each landing has a window and a metal bin door covering the *poubelle* 'trash shoot.' Each floor repeats the pattern of four apartments. Our apartment is the one between the elevator and the stairs on the fourth floor, but five flights up because of the ground floor.

As you enter our apartment from the hall our door opens to a small entry. On the left is an unusual bathroom for Europe because all the plain white fixtures are in one room. There is no water closet. All the fixtures are in line from the door – toilet, sink, bidet – and across the back, the tub. Behind the tub is the water heater and above the tub, a rectangular frame, two-and-a-half-by-four-feet with four clotheslines. The clothesline frame goes up and down by an attached pulley and rope.

Across from the sink sits a floor-to-ceiling built-in cupboard. The walls and cupboard are all thickly painted shiny vanilla. The kitchen, smaller than the bathroom, is placed straight across from the bathroom. Stepping into the kitchen, one can see the refrigerator sitting on a table on the right. The refrigerator is so small it is filled to capacity with a half-gallon of milk. The gas-stove straight in from the door stands on four legs, holding the oven about a foot off the floor; on top are four gas burners. Gas burners work about the same all over the world. The oven size is a foot across, a foot high, and a foot deep. That small, and it still bakes unevenly. A pumpkin pie has to be turned one-quarter turn every fifteen minutes, and bakes for over two hours. Next to the stove hangs a shallow, one-bowl sink, no stopper. I use a dishpan for washing dishes. Left of the sink is a warped sideboard attached to the wall. The size of the sideboard is about eight inches deep and a foot-and-a-half long. The warp makes it dip in the middle. It, and the walls, are of the same shiny vanilla color, but most of the paint has washed off the sideboard. Above the sideboard, the window has six thick panes of heavy rumpled glass, the two sides of which open into the room. A flat sill outside, the same size as the sideboard, is an additional winter refrigerator. Turning left, you face a closet of shelves containing an assortment of household utensils. One little step and you are back in the entry.

Across the entry from the front door is a large rectangular room with three tall windows. Classic French windows, six feet high; each window has two sides. Each side is a collection of framed panes of glass covered with a long lace curtain. Turning the knob in the middle unlatches the windows, and the two sides pull into the room. When the windows are closed, large, heavy, red velvet drapes can be pulled to create almost darkness. Two of the windows monopolize most of the north wall on your right. These two windows look to the street on which we live, Edouard Detaille. The view is mostly of parked cars and the apartment buildings across the street. These apartments look just like ours, made of concrete and built in the mid-1950s.

Edouard Detaille came to life one spring Saturday morning when a three-piece gypsy band and a dancing bear came down our street. I was so excited. Other apartment dwellers are throwing money so I try throwing some centimes real hard, but our window is about thirty feet from the street.

The window on the west end straight ahead looks out over rooftops and the hills heading toward Versailles. This window presents engaging, cloud-filled sunsets. Denver sits on latitude 39.43 north and Paris sits on latitude 48.52 north. This almost ten-degree difference is already big because in winter these sunsets take place in the late afternoon. Like in most European homes and apartments, the windows have shutters on the outside. Ours are the common multi-fold metal kind. I never get used to closing the shutters each night and opening them each morning. So they are open most of the time. In the summer, however, I close the shutters all the time, day and night, and leave the windows open. This lets the breeze blow in through the louvers.

The big room is eclectically furnished with a small hutch, a round table, two chairs, an end-table set, an armoire, a closet smaller than the armoire, and a built-in waist-high shelf along half of the south wall. There are two of what you might call couches. The couch/cot when performing as a couch has two large pillows leaned against the wall and two large pillows for a seat; each end folds up to become tall arms. When performing as a cot, the arms come down, level with the seat, and the wall pillows complete the cot. The couch/bed, clever for a studio, has a padded headboard-like structure, only, it fits along the side of the bed. This sideboard, upholstered with forest-green velvet-like material, has a matching cover that fits over the bed. When it is performing as a couch, it does so with a very wide seat.

In this cozy abode, with household items not good enough for a garage sale, we settle in to make a home.

The first matter needing our attention is getting married. No, wait. We need to get groceries, then get married. France, the number one place on earth for the arts of cooking and eating, and we have taken all our meals but one in the army snack bar. Why? Because we can afford it.

The army snack bar, a busy place serving breakfast, lunch, and dinner to all who form the line past the cafeteria-style preparations or ordering from the grill. Over time I become familiar with their inventory practices. I assure you, fresh hamburger buns are only ordered every six months. My life fills with numerous little inconveniences that soon become normal and then, an adorable way of life.

The American Legion Post #1 dishes up our meal the one night away from the snack bar that first week. I hunger for a big glass of cold milk. So I order milk with my dinner. No need to say cold when ordering milk. The glass set before me looks delicious. I pick it up and take a long swallow. Blah! It is room temperature and lumpy. Not good milk gone bad; good milk not homogenized and not refrigerated. A big surprise for the little girl from Colorado.

Al makes fewer than two hundred dollars a month when I arrive. We pay monthly rent of one hundred twenty dollars. To move into the apartment we pay three hundred and sixty dollars, or eighteen hundred francs. It breaks down this way: one twenty to the agent, one twenty for damage deposit, and one twenty for first month's rent. This took the better part of the money I brought with me. We also pay gas, electricity, and phone. We get around using the free army bus or the Paris metro. We purchase metro tickets a carnet (book of ten) at a time, which costs about two dollars. Both of us going somewhere and coming back uses up four tickets. Discretionary income or all the money left after we pay the bills we use for purchasing food. That puts eating in the category of luxury, not necessity.

The first couple of months in the apartment we struggle with money and concern about my getting lost. I really begin to suffer emotionally from cabin fever, and physically from inactivity.

I cannot shop in any of the army stores because of my civilian status. I do not get dependent status until the wedding day. After our initial trip to the commissary for basic supplies, Al picks up what we need at the small convenience store-like place in the snack bar building. This store opens at 10:00 A.M. One morning, after Al got off work from night shift at 8:00 A.M. he stayed in town to wait for the store to open and buy supplies. Desperate to get out and see people, I beg to come to town and just sit in the snack bar and have a Coke. This will cost two metro tickets, fifteen cents, and ten cents for a Coke. Al's answer to my request, "We cannot afford it."

This upsets me so much I take off for a walk. I plan to walk until after I know he will be home so he will worry. I figure that if I take careful note of my surroundings and concentrate on landmarks, I can find my way back home. I make the big mistake of setting out wearing slacks. Not sloppy slacks, but a nice, neat, dress slack. In 1964 Paris "nice" women do not wear slacks. Maybe on a Saturday morning for a picnic or country visits, slacks would be okay, but during the week, never, never, never. So while I stroll down by the river a car stops and the man inside says something and motions me to get in the car. I shake my head. He became quite insistent that I join him in his car. His obvious intentions cause me to scream at him in English, "I don't understand you!" I walk on and he drives off.

When I arrive back home I have accomplished what I intended. Al stands worried at the window. I should not have done this to him. He is working hard to manage our meager amount of money, and he is right, we cannot afford to spend a quarter.

Getting paid once a month when you don't have enough money to live really takes discipline. Lucky for me, Al is so fiscally responsible. Nevertheless, the first of every month we buy a T-bone steak. Only one. Al, the sweetheart, always lets me have the big side. After several months of doing this he looks at me curiously and says, "Don't you really know the difference?" Then he explains that the smaller side, the tenderloin, is a better cut of meat. I didn't care. I continue to claim the big side so I get more steak. Having T-bone steak the first of every month means we have spaghetti at the end of every month. I make a big pot of spaghetti and we re-heat it every day until payday. Months with thirty-one days mean eating really mushy spaghetti.

When Al is not at work, all he does is read. Living with a constant reader in one room, and all I do is read too. When Al is at work, he reads, so while I'm alone, I read. We have trouble saving because we buy so many magazines and paperback books. I suggest we make better use of the small library in the building with the snack bar. By the time we leave Paris Al has read every book in the Science Fiction section of this library.

I mentioned my problem with dyslexia and writing. Even though the public school system gave me a high school diploma, I do not read well. In this environment of no radio, no TV, no friends, no family, and one room, living with a constant reader is the best thing that ever happened to me. I read everything from *Tom Sawyer and Huckleberry Finn*, which I had not read as a child, to John Steinbeck's *East of Eden* which once I started, I couldn't put down. On library days we check out four or five books for Al and a book for me. When I finish my book and Al finishes all of his and mine, we have library day again. He reads my book when I am fixing dinner or something. So we both finish our reading at about the same time. Plus, he is also reading newspapers and magazines.

Letters I receive from family and friends often start with: "You are so lucky to be in such a glamorous place." No doubt about the correctness of this statement. I regret I did not take advantage of the opportunity as much as I should have. I feel I did not, partly because of money, partly because of immaturity, and partly because wherever you live, you fill your life with everyday chores, not tourist adventures.

I think about these letters and the view others have of me, while I am on my hands and knees scrubbing the floor. The kitchen, bath, and entry all have slate tile. This tile is unforgiving; if you drop anything breakable, it will shatter. The tile and a new large bottle of ketchup conspired to help me gain some maturity.

The bottle of ketchup sitting on top of the refrigerator leaps to the floor when the door shut. It hits with commanding force and explodes everywhere. In such a diminutive space, a large bottle of ketchup covers every possible surface. I take one look at this mess and run into the other room, throw myself on the bed and cry loud and hard. I cry for an extended time, then turn on my back and take a bit of time to feel sorry for myself. Then I ask myself, "Would you rather be here cleaning up the ketchup mess or back home going dancing and hanging out at the popular drive-in restaurant?" No, I do not want my teenage life back. A calm comes over me as I answer, "I had better get that mess cleaned up before it starts to dry. I am definitely where I want to be." This place, no matter how crummy, is my home, and deserves my loving care. I scrub the kitchen top to bottom, but still find a spot of ketchup here or there for weeks.

The floor in the big room is wood, set in a zigzag pattern. The boards have dried and shrunken. As much as half an inch gap between the boards in some places sit, ready to gobble tiny matter. Starting at the far end of the room with a broom, I gather some dirt, but cannot get to the other side of the room and collect the dirt into a dustpan because the dirt falls into the cracks.

The furnishing includes two rugs, four feet by six feet; they can be positioned to cover the biggest cracks. Both rugs have a pattern, but not the same pattern. They each display the colors red, gray, and black; or, the gray part might be white. Without a vacuum, I clean the rugs by dragging them one at a time over to one of the north windows, easing it a little at a time over the window rail. Each window has a ten-inch sill outside, a five-inch step up from inside, and a railing painted forest-green and fashioned of sturdy metal. The top piece of the railing is made of a four-inch round pipe attached to the outside of the building. Smaller, more decorative pieces attach the pipe to the sill. The top of the railing hits me just about the bend of my leg, below my hip. Once I carefully work the rug out the window, I maneuver it so I can hang onto the end and give it a shake. Once while doing this I let the rug pull me a little too far, and my feet lifted off the sill. I struggled back and regained my footing. My most ardent hope is that I am smart enough to let go of the rug if I do not recover my footing.

Our telephone sits in a nook in the wall of the entryway next to the bathroom door. The army requires us to have a telephone so they can call Al. For some reason I still remember the number: Molitor *soixante-dix vingt*. That is the exact way I remember it. If you want me to tell you it in English, I have to stop and translate it. Molitor is the name of a region. Years ago, in the United States, we also had region names at the beginning of our phone numbers. *Soixante-dix vingt* is sixty twenty or 6020. When the phone rings I pick up the receiver and say a word that sounds like "alloo wee." The other party, if speaking French, would hear me attempt, "*Ici* Molitor *soixante-dix vingt*" (here, in this place, Molitor sixty twenty).

I make one big mistake with the telephone. The beginning of 1965, three of the guys doing the same communications job as Al have rotated out of this assignment and have not been replaced. Army personnel perform this job for the army and the embassy because the State Department has a shortage of this skill. So embassies use army guys whenever possible. I would like to tell you more about Al's job, but because it has to do with communications of a classified nature, I knew very little about it, and you shouldn't know about it either.

Al's schedule has always been work six days on day shift, two days off. Work six days on evening shift, two days off. Work six days on night shift, two days off. Repeat. With only three guys left after the rotation, each one has to take a shift and work it everyday. Al has the evening shift. He can stay home two days a week, but he has to be at home in the event that they call. They always call.

On one of his stay-at-home days I wait to see if he would be called in before I make dinner. They didn't call, so I started dinner. The phone rings just as I am placing dinner on the table. I answer it. I usually recognized the voice of the caller. This time I didn't. The voice says, "Is Al there?" I flippantly reply, "Yes, but he can't come to work. He is about to eat dinner." The voice said, "I beg your pardon?" This should have put me on notice, but I push my foot deeper into my mouth and say, "Yes, but he can't come to work. He is about to eat dinner." The voice, "May I speak to him?" I say yes and hand the phone to Al. Now, I can only hear Al's side but it goes like this, "Yes, sir . . . yes, sir . . . yes, sir." I know I have made a mistake. I didn't know how big a mistake until Al got back home after the call. The man to whom I gave my mouthy declaration was an aide to Dean Rusk. Dean Rusk served as secretary of state for Presidents Kennedy and Johnson. The aide was calling Al because the State Department needed Al at the embassy.

Doing the Tasks

Now that we have a home base, let me explain the logistics of the places we go to the most.

During World War II the Nazis built a communication center at 29 rue la Perouse, three blocks from the Arc de Triomphe. The communication center is made of very thick reinforced concrete with no windows. All of the exterior sides are coarse, unrefined concrete. This building could supposedly withstand a direct hit from a bomb of that era. The French landowner rents the building to the United States Forces because of the prohibitive cost of tearing it down. The GIs quite descriptively call it the BlockHouse. Al lived inside this fortress until the night of my phone call from the States. I have trouble understanding how Al could tolerate living and working in this place. Here again, it has mostly to do with money.

The living quarters in the BlockHouse consist of two rooms. One room always remains dark and has eight cots, four on each side and a very large noisy fan at the far end running constantly. The communications center is active twenty-four hours a day, seven days a week, so there are always some workers sleeping. The sleeping room is located off a lounging room. The lounging room contains two couches, some end tables, and a toaster. I hear some wild stories about food preparation on and in the toaster. I describe these rooms from hearsay. Only people with a top-secret clearance can enter the building.

From the street a large opening, with no door, begins a tunnel that extends clear through the side of the building. At the other end of the tunnel is an open courtyard surrounded by high walls. In the middle of the courtyard sits a fifty-five-gallon drum used to burn the trash. I walked in and surprised the trash burners once and they surprised me because they carried guns to burn the trash. All this trash is top-secret teletype. Several steps into the tunnel from the street, on the right is a smaller opening to a cramped corridor that curves to the left. If someone exits as you enter, you have to squeeze past. At the end of the short hall begins a flight of steps, which is the only way into and out of the building. Just before the steps, there is a guard desk behind which always sits an MP (Military Police). Once I begged the MP to allow me to go up one flight of stairs to use the toilet. I really had to go badly. He had to go with me and wait outside the door. I remember only seeing darkness. Maybe they turned the lights out because I was there. Other than this one time, I never went past the guard's desk. When Al went away on temporary duty, I would go to the MP, ask him to call the com-center, and ask anyone there to bring me my mail.

Our most used army facility is an art deco five-story building located a good walk from the BlockHouse and half a block off the Champs Elysee on rue Marbeuf. We call this multi-use army building just plain Marbeuf. It houses the aforementioned snack bar, library, and convenience store. Also found in the Marbeuf building is the newsstand, the dentist, the doctor, and officers' club. From our apartment we walk three blocks to the metro and take about a half-hour ride to the Franklin D. Roosevelt stop then walk a couple of blocks to rue Marbeuf. For Al to go to work he takes the same metro, but two stops before the Franklin D stop, at stop Trocadero, he changes to another line and goes two more stops to stop Kleber and walks three blocks to the BlockHouse.

Several miles west of Paris is a place called Chateau bel manoir. This chateau housed the office of General Eisenhower while he commanded Allied Forces in Europe after the war.

I was born six days before "D" day, the Normandy invasion. So I felt World War II a part of long-ago history. But for many of the people who lived through it, twenty years is not that long ago.

On the land around the chateau, the army built a shopping center. This troop service sight provides another snack bar, the PX, a beauty and barbershop, a tailor, the cleaners, and the commissary.

From our apartment we walk the same three blocks, as if going to the metro. But just before the metro we turn left and cross the street for the army bus stop. The bus takes about a half-hour to get to bel manoir. Staying on the bus for another half-hour delivers us to the end of the line at Camp des loges. Camp des loges, the main army base for the whole Paris area is located northwest of Paris, close to St. Denis. Camp des Loges has everything already mentioned, and more. It has all the stores and services I already listed plus churches, officers' housing, training areas, and enlisted men's barracks. It also has the enlisted men's club, a very small laundromat, and all the other things you might find on any army post in the United States.

We think we have selected a smart location to live because we are close to all the transportation we will be using in our daily lives.

We move into our apartment with my suitcases, Al's duffel bag and laundry bag, the boxes I mailed, and an old record player. Al has a day off and we take the army bus to the commissary at bel manoir. A commissary is the army's version of a supermarket. We use the little money we have left from the stash I brought to buy groceries. We need everything from salt and pepper to that night's dinner. When we finish we have six or seven paper shopping bags with twisted handles filled to the top. The two of us grapple these bags onto the bus. Returning home, we ask the driver to let us off the bus before we reach the intersection where we boarded the bus to go to the store. We took a wrong turn after exiting the bus prematurely. Carrying all the heavy bags, we are lost. We have high expectations that a turn at the end of each block will deliver us to familiar ground. The pain in my arms, legs, and back from carrying those bags is about to overwhelm me. I suggest I stay with the bags while Al locates the apartment, but the possibility exists that he will then not be able to relocate me. I know I truly cannot move one more block. The next turn we find our home. Now, it really is our home and we can always find it. We find it even decades later after the Peripherique is built and the landscape around Port De St Cloud is altered.

Okay, now we have groceries, let's get married. I have explained the six days on two days off schedule. Every possible day off we spend in pursuit of the papers we need first from the army, then from the French government. I can do nothing without Al while dealing with the army. My status as a civilian and not even a dependent means that I am trespassing on any army property if I am without an escort. I do the little housework needed for our tiny place and write letters home. I do all the meal preparation. I like to think it is due to our budget more than my culinary skills but we are both losing weight.

For entertainment we play canasta. We play this card game, which uses two decks, so much, that to break the routine we try playing it with three decks. The *Hoyle's Book of Games* becomes our best friend while playing canasta and other card games, as it saves many an argument. Our original Hoyle book fell to pieces from overuse, so for our thirtieth wedding anniversary I bought us a new Hoyle book to get us through the next thirty years.

We ask our families for board games for Christmas, which gave us a break from canasta. When money allows, we go to the movies. The theaters on the Champs Elysees show American movies in English, with French sub-titles.

Going to the movies in France has forever spoiled us for movie theaters in the United States. The French moviegoers are so quiet and polite that U.S. movie theaters sound to us more like WWF fans gone wild.

The army has a list of tasks we must complete in order to get married. I don't know why they won't give us a copy of the list. We report to the orderly room in the Marbeuf building and receive instruction on a task. After completing that task we return with the proof of its fulfillment. The reward for this achievement is a directive for the next task. Frustration builds because of the back and forth, and not knowing the number of tasks. The orderly room and all other offices in which we need to conduct our business keep strict hours of nine to six or eight to five, weekdays only. If Al's two days off fall on the weekend, a fortnight can pass with no marriage activity. We make every effort to actualize our goals in the early afternoon on the days Al works evenings, and early in the morning when he gets off after working all night. If the task requires us to travel to Camp de Loges, it takes all day and we have to wait for a day off. While trying to complete many tasks we find offices closed, the person we need to see not available, or that we need to make an appointment at their convenience.

The first and easiest task I accomplished on my arrival was by carrying the notarized parental permission. I believe the army is fond of having this task first. If the folks say no, the army doesn't have to move forward with Al's request for marriage permission.

The next task they line up is a blood test for STDs (sexually transmitted diseases). The army found over the years that if a soldier wants to marry a woman in a foreign land and this type of blood test comes back positive, many times the soldier will change his mind. We each have a blood test. Wait several days for the results. Return the results. Next task: see the priest at Camp de Loges.

Now it is October, I have been here over a month and we have found a day to go to Camp de Loges. The priest is a pretty easygoing guy. He takes pity on our difficulty of reaching him for the several sessions of required counseling and gives us a book to read about marriage. He tells us we must have our banns of marriage* read at our home parish.

We write to Al's mom and ask her to arrange to have our banns read. She attends Mass for the three Sundays of the reading and got us the church bulletin in which the banns are printed so we can have them for a keepsake. The second Sunday of their reading was the first Sunday after the assassination of President Kennedy. She is unable to get a bulletin that Sunday because of the crowds attending church.

We understood about the crowds, as we have lost a task day that week to attend a special mass for President Kennedy. The American Catholic Church located close to the Arc de Triomphe on Avenue de Friedland held the mass on a weekday, and it was packed.

They say everyone over a certain age in November 1963 remembers where he or she was when they heard the news that the president had been shot. The time difference between the States and Europe means the event happened in the evening for us. Al is working days so when our phone rings, it awakens us. I answer the phone. Ray, calling from the BlockHouse, gives us the news. His landlord heard about the shooting on her nightly TV news. She rushed to Ray's room to inform him. He then went to the BlockHouse to see what messages were coming from the States. I think he is teasing me when he calls us, and I tell him I don't think it is funny. I hear his voice break as he assures me it is not a joke. I know this is grave. I hand the phone to Al.

Next morning, my hunger for information ravages. Al and I decide I will come into town and join him for lunch. My metro ride into Paris is agonizing. I feel like everyone recognizes me as an American and gapes at me. I know nothing of what has happened. A man is reading a newspaper on the train with six-inch headlines, "*KENNEDY ASSASSINER.*" When I arrive at Marbeuf all the *New York Herald Tribune* and *Stars and Stripes* newspapers are sold out. I remove papers from the trashcans to read about the tragedy.

I have had some long lonely days, but three months has flown by. It is now the end of November and the task assignment to complete is a session with the adjutant general. The adjutant general is the army's lawyer. This requires another trip to Camp de Loges. We call to make an appointment and find we have to make the appointment in person so the clerk can record Al's ID. Now, it becomes two trips to Camp de Loges. The reason these trips take all day is the hassle about my civilian condition. When the bus enters Camp de Loges we have to get off and register me as a visitor and get me a visitor's pass. When we exit we must turn in my visitor's pass to be sure I have left the premises. The bus doesn't wait while we register, so we can't ride to our destination; we walk. Al has to wear his uniform while visiting post. Many cars pass us as we walk, and Al has to keep his eye on the cars because some of them carry insignia, which requires that Al salute the car. Army life takes getting used to.

We finally meet the adjutant general. This relaxed, happy, and charming man listens closely to our plight. Then he throws his head back and with *a-ha ha ha* tells us, "You won't be getting married this year." I think he must be joking. He doesn't understand how hard we are working on this project.

The adjutant general laughs even more as he explains to us the requirement for our seeing him. When a soldier wants to get married, he (the adjutant general) must tell the wife-to-be (me) how to become an American citizen. I am a citizen by birth, but the orderly room still needs a compliance letter from this man.

However, this did not turn out to be an idle task. He takes a meticulous look at all our paperwork. He tells us some of our documents would need notarized translation, most obviously the parental permission. He generously took care of this for us.

I don't remember the cost of an airmail stamp, but we couldn't afford to send Christmas cards via airmail. Boat mail took four to six weeks.

With full confidence we would be married before Christmas, I sent Christmas cards the second week of November to friends and family from the two of us. Vexed, Al's mom wrote that after receiving the Christmas cards everyone assumed we were married, so she allowed that belief to stand. She had asked me before I left if we planned to get two apartments. I told her our financial situation would not allow for that, and alone, thousands of miles from home, any questionable behavior would not be ruled in or out because of the number of apartments. My grandmother, exasperated with our circumstance, wrote to me in no uncertain terms that I must sleep on the couch. In a recent discussion with my cousin, she told me that most of my extended family kept a hush hush demeanor about me. My dear sweet mother remained stoic, yet helpful and polite. She asks if it would be possible for us to go to England and get married. I guess she thought people speaking the same language could expedite the process. She may have been right, because we are dealing with the military, and they not only have their own language, they have their own way of life as well, which, whenever possible, should exclude spouses, most especially spouses from a foreign country. If a soldier is seeking permission to marry while stationed in a foreign country, he must be planning to marry a foreigner.

* In order to check the increase of clandestine marriages, the Council of Trent decreed (Sess. XXIV, de ref. matr., c. i) that before the celebration of any marriage the names of the contracting parties should be announced publicly in the church during the solemnization of mass by their own parish priest on three consecutive holy days: Waterworth, The Canons, and Decrees of the Sacred and Ecumenical Council of Trent, London, 1848, 196 ssq. Such a publication, of course, can be made only at the request of the parties themselves, and after the parish priest is aware of their mutual free consent. Moreover, the parish priest cannot refuse to publish the banns except for reasons stated in the canon law. If the contracting parties refuse to consent to the publication of the banns, the parish priest cannot assist at their marriage, and where the Tridentine legislation does not obtain, he is bound to warn them not to attempt marriage elsewhere. In

the course of time this Tridentine decree has given occasion to more specific interpretation, regularly and primarily applicable where the decree has been promulgated. Among the more important authentic decisions are the following: The proper (own) parish priest of persons intending marriage is he in whose parish both (or one of) the contracting parties have a true domicile or quasi-domicile, i.e. a fixed residence or one that can be legally constructed as such. When both parties permanently reside in the same parish, no difficulty can arise as to the parish priest whose right and duty it is to publish the banns. But it may happen that one party resides, or that both parties have each more than one domicile or quasi-domicile, in which case the publication of the banns should occur. Regularly speaking, in every parish where at the time of the marriage the parties retain such domicile or quasi-domicile.

6 December 1963

SUBJECT: Application for permission to marry

TO: Commanding Officer, 275th Signal Co, APO 163, US Forces

    In compliance with USAREUR Regulation No 608-61, I certify that on the above date SP-4 ALBERT R. ENDERIE, RA 17 628 160 and PATRICIA L. JUMP reported to my office and were counseled by me in compliance with USAREUR Regulation.

ALBERT B. OSBORNE
Dept of Army Attorney
Judge Advocate Division
Hq Seine Area Command
APO 163, US Forces

Certificate given in lieu of Form 3217

APPLICATION FOR PERMISSION TO MARRY
(AR 608-61)

SEE INSTRUCTIONS ON REVERSE SIDE

DATE: 6 December 1963

SECTION I - PERSONAL DATA OF APPLICANT

1. APPLICANT (Last name - First name - Middle name): Enderle Albert Raymond
2. GRADE: E-4
3. SERVICE NUMBER: RA17628160
4. DATE OF BIRTH: 18 November 1943
5. COMPLETE MILITARY ADDRESS: 275th Sig Co Svc, APO 163
6. ROTATION DATE: 28 March 1965
7. EXPIRATION TERM OF SERVICE DATE: 18 April 1965
8. LEGAL RESIDENCE (Number, Street, City, State): 5967 Flower, Arvada, Colorado
9. NATIONALITY: American
10. RACE: Caucasian
11. LENGTH OF PERIOD OF COURTSHIP: Two years
12. APPROXIMATE DATE MARRIAGE TO BE PERFORMED: 30 May 1964
13. PLACE WHERE MARRIAGE CEREMONIES WILL BE PERFORMED (City and Country): Paris, France
14. PREVIOUS MARRIAGES: None

SECTION II - PERSONAL DATA OF PROSPECTIVE SPOUSE

15. PROSPECTIVE SPOUSE (Last name - First name - Middle name): Jump Patricia Lou
16. DATE OF BIRTH: 30 May 1944
17. RACE: Caucasian
18. NATIONALITY: American
19. PRESENT ADDRESS: 9 rue Edouard Detaille, Paris, France
20. LEGAL ADDRESS (Permanent Address): 5871 Balsam, Arvada, Colorado
21. PREVIOUS MARRIAGES: None

22. DEPENDENTS OF PROSPECTIVE SPOUSE

NAME	AGE	RELATIONSHIP	ADDRESS
None			

SECTION III - REMARKS

24. (This space is for entry of information which may be required by local commander but not otherwise provided for and continuation of information required in other items where space is insufficient.)

a. The provisions of AR 600-240 and USAREUR Reg 608-30 have been explained to me and I understand their meaning.
b. I understand that a request for an extension fo foreign service tour solely on the basis of incomplete action on my marriage application will not be favorably considered.
c. I certify that I am not over twenty-one (21) years of age.
d. I have in excess of $300.00 in my savings account.

SECTION IV - STATEMENT OF APPLICANT

25. I HAVE INVESTIGATED THE CONDITIONS WHICH MUST BE SATISFIED FOR MY PROSPECTIVE SPOUSE AND CHILDREN, IF ANY, TO GAIN ENTRY INTO THE UNITED STATES FOR PERMANENT RESIDENCE AND I AM PREPARED TO EXERCISE MY RIGHTS TO GAIN SUCH ENTRY FOR MY PROSPECTIVE SPOUSE AND CHILDREN. I UNDERSTAND THAT IT IS MY RESPONSIBILITY TO INITIATE AN APPLICATION FOR NONQUOTA IMMIGRATION VISA SUBSEQUENT TO DATE OF MARRIAGE.

26. ENTRANCE INTO THE UNITED STATES OR TERRITORY IS NOT CONTEMPLATED FOR THE FOLLOWING REASONS: (If applicable only)

27. I [ ] AM [X] AM NOT RELATED TO MY PROSPECTIVE SPOUSE BY BLOOD. (If positive, explain degree of relationship.)

28. I UNDERSTAND MY MORAL OBLIGATIONS WITH RESPECT TO PROVIDING A HOME AND ADEQUATE SUPPORT FOR MY PROSPECTIVE SPOUSE AND DEPENDENTS, IF ANY, IN THE EVENT MARRIAGE IS CONSUMMATED. NECESSARY ARRANGEMENTS HAVE BEEN MADE BY ME TO PROVIDE FOR MY PROSPECTIVE SPOUSE AND DEPENDENTS, IF ANY, IN SUCH A MANNER AS TO INSURE THAT THEY DO NOT BECOME A PUBLIC BURDEN UPON THE UNITED STATES OR GOVERNMENTAL AGENCIES OF ANY OTHER COUNTRY WITHIN THE FORESEEABLE FUTURE.

29. I UNDERSTAND THAT I AM LIABLE FOR PROSECUTION UNDER THE APPROPRIATE MILITARY REGULATIONS FOR FALSE OR MISLEADING INFORMATION SUBMITTED IN CONNECTION WITH THIS APPLICATION.

30. I AGREE THAT IF MY PROSPECTIVE SPOUSE OR MYSELF CHANGE OUR INTENTION TO ENTER INTO THIS MARRIAGE, PRIOR TO RECEIPT OF AUTHORITY THEREFOR, I WILL NOTIFY MY UNIT COMMANDER IMMEDIATELY SO THAT PROCESSING OF THIS APPLICATION MAY BE STOPPED.

DATE: 7 December 63
SIGNATURE OF APPLICANT: Albert R. Enderle

INSTRUCTIONS

1. The following supporting documents, as applicable, must be procured by the applicant and submitted in a single copy with the application:

   a. Notarized statement of consent of the parent or legal guardian responsible for the custody of prospective alien spouse who is below the legal age for marriage in the nation or locality where marriage is to be performed.

   b. Notarized statement of consent of the parent or legal guardian responsible for the custody of applicant if under 21 years of age.

   c. Final divorce decree, annulment or other satisfactory documentary evidence of the termination of any previous marriage by divorce, annulment or death. Copy submitted must be a certified or true copy issued by the appropriate governmental agency or official having custody of such records.

   d. Birth certificates of both parties and their dependents. Copies submitted must be certified or true copies issued by the appropriate governmental agency or official having custody of such records.

2. When the space under any item is insufficient for entry of the required information, reference will be made to Section III. "Remarks" and entry of information continued therein. Section III. "Remarks" will contain a cross reference to the item being continued. Additional sheets may be added as required and should be appropriately identified.

SECTION V - ACTION OF APPLICANT'S IMMEDIATE COMMANDER

TO: Commanding Officer
1st Signal Group
APO 58, US Forces

FROM: Commanding Officer
275th Sig Co (Svc)
APO 163, US Forces

1. RECOMMEND [X] APPROVAL [ ] DISAPPROVAL

2. REMARKS

   a. The applicant has been thoroughly counseled relative to the proposed marriage.

   b. Birth certificate of each party have been examined and the requirements of par 7b (1) and (3), USAREUR Regulation 608-30 have been met.

   c. Applicant has no action pending under AR 600-31.

TYPED NAME AND GRADE OF COMMANDER OR DESIGNATED REPRESENTATIVE
MORTON L BLAUSTEIN, Maj, SigC
Commanding

SIGNATURE

SECTION VI - ACTION COMMANDER HAVING CUSTODY OF MILITARY PERSONNEL RECORDS

TO: Commanding Officer
1st Signal Group
APO 58, US Forces

FROM: Personnel Officer
275th Sig Co (Svc)
APO 163, US Forces

1. RECOMMEND [X] APPROVAL [ ] DISAPPROVAL

2. APPLICANT [X] HAS [ ] HAS NOT BEEN COUNSELLED BY MILITARY CHAPLAIN AND LEGAL ASSISTANCE OFFICER IN ACCORDANCE WITH THE PROVISIONS OF PARAGRAPH 2b (1) (2) AR

3. APPLICANT [X] HAS [ ] HAS NOT BEEN EXAMINED BY A MEDICAL OFFICER AND FOUND FREE FROM COMMUNICABLE DISEASES, INFECTIOUS VENEREAL DISEASE AND ACTIVE TUBERCULOSIS

4. I [X] HAVE [ ] HAVE NOT DISCUSSED WITH THE APPLICANT HIS FINANCIAL OBLIGATIONS IN CONNECTION WITH THE PROPOSED MARRIAGE AND HE HAS SATISFIED ME THAT ADEQUATE ARRANGEMENTS HAVE OR CAN BE MADE FOR THE SUPPORT OF HIS PROSPECTIVE SPOUSE.

5. REMARKS: (If disapproval is recommended or if either paragraph 2, 3, or 4, is answered in the negative or with exception, explain fully below. Attach additional sheet when required.)

TYPED NAME AND GRADE OF COMMANDER OR DESIGNATED REPRESENTATIVE
EUGENE J DOBRZELECKI JR, 1Lt, SigC, PersO

SIGNATURE

CERTIFICATE OF PERSONNEL OFFICER FOR MARRIAGES IN FRANCE
CERTIFICAT DELIVRE PAR LE CHEF DU PERSONNEL POUR LES MARIAGES EN FRANCE

NAME / Nom	GRADE / Grade	SN/PP NO / Numéro mtr/passeport
ENDERLE, Albert Raymond	SP4 E4	RA 17 628 160

PRESENT ORGANIZATION/PLACE OF EMPLOYMENT	CITY AND STATE OF RESIDENCE	DATE AND PLACE OF BIRTH (City & State)
275th Signal Company (Svc) APO 163, New York, New York	5967 Flower St., Arvada, Colorado	18 Nov 43 Council Bluffs, Iowa

NAME OF PROPOSED SPOUSE	PRESENT ADDRESS (City and Dept)	DATE AND PLACE OF BIRTH (City and State)
Patricia L Jump	#9 Rue Elouard Detaille Paris 16, France	Arvada, Colorado

[X] SINGLE (Célibataire) [ ] WIDOWED (Veuf) [ ] DIVORCED (Divorcé)	NAME OF FORMER SPOUSE IF WIDOWED: NA	DATE AND PLACE OF DEATH (City and State): NA

COMMANDER GRANTING AUTHORITY FOR MARRIAGE	PLACE AUTHORITY GRANTED	DATE
Commanding Officer Hq 1st Signal Group, APO 58 NY NY	Orleans, France	8 Jan 64

MARRIAGE WILL BE ACCOMPLISHED PRIOR TO — DATE: 31 Jan 64

Je soussigné, délégué du Commandant en Chef des Forces Armées américaines en Europe, dûment habilité, certifie sur le vu des pièces officielles en ma possession, que la personne désignée ci-dessus est membre des Forces Armées américaines/employé civil des Forces Armées américaines, que les renseignements fournis ci-dessus sont exacts. Je certifie en outre que conformément aux lois civiles des Etats-Unis il peut contracter mariage sous réserve des dispositions legislatives de son Etat de résidence pouvant imposer des restrictions sur le mariage.

I the undersigned delegate of the Commander in Chief of the United States Army in Europe duly authorized for this purpose certify according to the official records in my possession that the above mentioned applicant is a member of the forces or civilian employee of the Forces of the United States, and that the above information is correct. I further certify that in conformity with the laws of the United States he has civil capacity to contract marriage, subject to the provisions of any law of the above named state of residence which may impose restrictions on the marriage.

SIGNED: EDGE. E J DORZELECKI JR
1st Lt, SigC
Personnel Officer

SUPPLEMENTAL INFORMATION / RENSEIGNEMENTS SUPPLEMENTAIRES

	NAME	LIVING/DECEASED	NATIONALITY
FATHER	Raymond A. Enderle	[X] Living	American
MOTHER	MAIDEN NAME: Arlyne M. BeBoer	[X] Living	American

	ADDRESS	OCCUPATION
FATHER	5967 Flower St., Arvada, Colorado	Vice President, Colo., Serum Co. Denver, Colo.
MOTHER	5967 Flower St., Arvada, Colorado	Housewife

AE FORM 3203 13 DEC 62   PREVIOUS EDITION OF THIS FORM IS OBSOLETE.

HEADQUARTERS
1ST SIGNAL GROUP
APO 58, US FORCES

AEZQ-A

8 January 1964

SUBJECT: Approval of Application for Permission to Marry

THRU:
Via: Commanding Officer
       275th Signal Company (Svc)
       APO 163, US Forces

TO:
A: SP4 Albert R. ENDERLE
       275th Signal Company (Svc)
       APO 163, US Forces

1. Your application for permission to marry **Miss Patricia L. JUMP** is approved.
   Votre demande d'autorisation de mariage avec **Melle Patricia L. JUMP** est acceptee.

Marriage must be performed in compliance with the laws of the country in which the ceremony is performed. This approval is valid for six months.
Le mariage doit etre accompli en accord avec les lois du pays dans lequel la ceremonie est celebre. Cette approbation est valable pour 6 mois.

2. Approval of a proposed marriage to an alien in no way confers either United States citizenship or insures receipt of a visa for entry into the United States for an alien spouse after marriage. Such action is within the jurisdiction of the appropriate United States Immigration authorities.
L'approbation d'un mariage propose avec un etranger ne confere aucunement le droit de citoyennete americaine de meme qu'il n'assure pas la possession d'un visa d'entree aux Etats Unis pour une epouse etrangere. Une telle action ressort de la juridiction des autorites appropriees de l'Immigration Americaine.

3. You must contact your unit personnel section and confer with a legal assistance officer regarding action to secure a visa for your dependents at least six months before your departure from your organization.
Vous devez contacter le bureau du personnel de votre unite et conferer avec un officier juridique concernant l'action a prendre pour obtenir un visa a votre famille, au moins 6 mois avant votre depart de l'organization.

FOR THE COMMANDER:

1 Incl
Marriage Application &
Allied Papers

CHARLES E. FAGAN
2d Lt, SigC
Asst Adjutant

Visas

IT IS THE RESPONSIBILITY OF THE PASSPORT BEARER
TO OBTAIN NECESSARY VISAS

RÉPUBLIQUE FRANÇAISE
PRÉFECTURE de POLICE
Direction de la Police Générale

Nom JUMP
Prénoms Patricia Lou
Visa de **Régularisation** N°
Valable jusqu'au

Taxe perçue 110 F Reçu N° 5469
Fait à PARIS, le 27 JANV 1964
Pour le PRÉFET DE POLICE
P/ le Directeur de la Police Générale,
le Chef du 5° Bureau

L'ORÉAL
de Paris
DIPLÔME
Spécialiste PERMANENTE
Patricia Enderle

"GUESDON"
10, rue Geoffroy Marie
PARIS (9:) tél.PRO.81-27

RÉPUBLIQUE
FRANÇAISE
★ 10
POSTES
MG 4873

30 I 64 = PARIS-48 =

Monsieur R. ENDERLE
9 rue Ed. Detaille
BOULOGNE   seine

Extrait de l'Acte de Mariage N° 7

Le huit février mil neuf cent soixante quatre, devant Nous ont comparu publiquement en la maison commune ...... heure ......

ÉPOUX

Nom et prénoms : ENDERLE — Gilbert Raymond

Né à Council Bluffs, État d'Iowa (États-Unis d'Amérique) Le dix-huit novembre mil neuf cent quarante trois

Fils de (1) Raymond Anthony ENDERLE
et de (1) Arlyne Neva DEBOER son épouse

(2) consentants par acte authentique
(3)

Contrat de mariage : Les futurs conjoints ont déclaré (4) : qu'il n'a

ÉPOUSE

Nom et prénoms : JUMP — Patricia Lou

Née à Arvada, État du Colorado (États-Unis d'Amérique) Le trente mai mil neuf cent quarante quatre

Fille de (1) Ernest Arthur JUMP décédé
et de (1) Nava TRINE sa veuve

(2) consentante par acte authentique
(3)

pas été fait de contrat de mariage

Signatures des Conjoints

Délivré conforme au registre le 8 février 1964
L'Officier d'État Civil :

MENTIONS MARGINALES (A)

(A) Divorce, jugement déclarant nul le mariage, jugement rectificatif.

MAIRIE DE BOULOGNE-BILLANCOURT

1re DIVISION
Bureau de l'Etat Civil

ANNÉE _____ 1964

N° DU REGISTRE

MR N° 71

ENDERLE
et
JUMP

EXTRAIT DU REGISTRE
DES ACTES DE MARIAGE

Le huit Février mil neuf cent soixante quatre, acte de mariage de Albert Raymond E N D E R L E, soldat de l'armée américaine, né à Council Bluffo, Etat d'Iowa (Etats Unis d'Amérique) le dix huit Novembre mil neuf cent quarante trois, domicilié à Arvada, Etat d Colorado, Etats Unis d'Amérique, et résidant à Boulogne-Billancou 9 Rue Edouard Detaille, fils de Raymond Anthony ENDERLE, et de Arlyne Neva DEBOER, son épouse, D'UNE PART. - ET: Patricia Lou J U M P, coiffeuse, née à Arvada, Etat du Colorado (Etats Unis d'Amérique) le trente Mai mil neuf cent quarante quatre, domicili à Denver, Etat du Colorado (Etats Unis d'Amérique) et résidant à Boulogne-Billancourt, 9 Rue Edouard Detaille, fille de Ernest Arther JUMP, décédé, et de Nava TRINE, sa veuve, D'AUTRE PART.- Sans contrat de mariage- Suivent les signatures -

Pour extrait conforme,
Boulogne-Billancourt, le quinze Décembre mil neuf
cent soixante quatre,

L'officier de l'état-civil délégué,

Military Ordinariate
United States of America
30 EAST FIFTY-FIRST STREET
NEW YORK 22, N. Y.

Certificate of Marriage

ALBERT RAYMOND ENDERLE
and PATRICIA LOU JUMP
were lawfully MARRIED on the 8th day of Feb., 1964

according to the Rite of the Catholic Church

at February-Camp Des Loges Post Chapel, Reverend Martin F. Buckley
officiating in the presence of Robert R. Morones
and Janine Perreau-Saussine witnesses.

The undersigned hereby attests that the foregoing is a correct transcript derived from the record as it appears in the Marriage Register of the Military Ordinariate.

In testimony whereof I have affixed my signature and the seal of the Military Ordinariate on Feb. 25, 1964

(L. S.)
ah
Record No. 204371

J. F. Marbach
Signature

Block house built by Nazis, 29 rue la Perouse.
Three blocks from Arc de Triomphe.

Al & Pat on steps of Mairie Mayor's Office, Baulogne-Billancourt.

Janine & Speed on steps of Mairie Mayor's Office, Baulogne-Billancourt.

Al & Pat, Chapel at Camp de loges

Janine-Pat-Al-Robert, Chapel at Camp de loges

Pat & Al, First anniversary, Lido

Al & Pat, Twenty fifth Anniversary, Bateaux Mouches

Gasthaus in Linggries, Germany – Honeymoon

Shocked by Embassy, Shocked by Electricity

Al and Ray are fast friends before I arrive. To describe Ray, I have to use the word sweetheart. All the sayings like "wouldn't hurt a fly" and "would give you the shirt off his back" apply to Ray. Raised in a working class neighborhood in Cleveland, Ray comes from a strong Catholic family. Al asks him to be the best man at our wedding. Ray is engaged to his longtime girlfriend. She awaits his homecoming as they have planned a large, family-filled church wedding as soon as he returns. His yearning for her surrounds him. He vows to remain true to her in spite of other GIs taunting him to accompany them to Pigalle or some other sleazy Paris haunt. The extra pounds that cling to him give him a cuddly appearance. Army units notorious for handing out nicknames have labeled him Meat. I call him Ray.

Benny Montgomery, another close friend, is way older than the rest of us. He must be all of twenty-five or – six. Montgomery was drafted. He left behind a lovely wife who writes him constantly and seals all the letters with big red lipstick kisses. He is a shy and quiet guy from Alabama and takes a lot of heckles about his letters.

In the military everyone has their last name on their shirt, so most everyone is called by their last name. Lin Amey, another chum, is from Colorado so we have a natural bond with him. Amey lost a front tooth in a fight before I arrived. The army dentist, in no hurry to complete the repair, leaves Amey putting his hand up or pulling his lip down when he talks. This makes it hard to understand him. Placement of the new tooth creates a marvelous transformation. Amey has a fabulous smile.

We got turkey for Thanksgiving and it cooked all day in the little oven. Amey and Montgomery are our guests for Thanksgiving dinner. I don't know why they were selected, but it probably had something to do with work schedules. Our apartment, furnished with only two chairs, are offered to our guests. I was going to sit on the kitchen stool but Amey insisted he take the stool and I have the chair. Al sat on his duffel bag filled three-quarters full and turned on end.

I found a bag of breadcrumbs with herbs so I figured I would just stuff them into the bird. A guy we call Cigar asks me how I make the dressing. I told him I have never made dressing. I told him about this bag of crumbs and herbs that I planned to use to fill up the cavity. His cooking skills are well known among our crowd. He grabs paper and pen and writes a list of ingredients and directions for a delicious dressing recipe I have since used for years. I still have his original note covered with butter stains and tucked into a cookbook.

I don't know Cigar's real name. He is air force, not army. He doesn't work at the BlockHouse. Military personnel are divided into two lots. The lifers, who will stay in the service for twenty years or more, and the draftees or joiners, just putting in their three or four years to fulfill their service obligation. Cigar is the former, Ray, Montgomery and Amey are all the latter. Then everyone is refereed to as being "new" (newly arrived) or a "short timer." A short timer is someone who has only a short time before being scheduled to return to the States and be discharged or reassigned. Ray holds the record for being a short timer longer than anyone else. On any given day he can tell you how many days he has left in country. He really wants to get home to his girl. I know so little about all these people, but they are trusted friends. Our small community is like a lifeboat. We have no control over who is in the boat, but we are all dependent on each other.

Never in my whole life before or after living in Paris have I made such good friends in such a short time. I could call on any one in our circle for help or a favor at any time. Amey and Lyles (I'll introduce you to Horace Lyles later) are the only ones with whom we have kept in contact. Any of the others can knock on my door tomorrow and receive a big hug and a "come on in."

I arrived the first of September, and now the calendar reads the end of November. A passport allows a ninety-day visit; after that time, without a visa, the visitor becomes a lawbreaker. I stop by the American Embassy, located on the northwest side of Place de la Concorde. It sits in a nice garden; many bushes separate the front from the street. I walk in the front door past the marine guard. An expansive lobby opens before me. The place reminds me of an elaborate old bank. Windows like teller windows wait opposite the front door. I approach a window tended by a middle-aged woman with dyed auburn hair. I explain my plight of exceeding my three months' stay. She asks, "Why are you here in France?" I tell her I have come to marry my American military boyfriend. She waves her hand. "Military, we can't keep track of all you military people." I am not military, but she doesn't seem to understand that. I should have explained that since I am not military to the military, how could I be military to the embassy? Instead, I stare through the bars at her face with a questioning look on my face. She shrugs and gives another wave of dismissal. I know this must be wrong. I think she should at least give me some advice about what I might be risking. My youth, innocence, and ignorance keep me from standing up to this civil servant whose job it is to help me. I turn and walk out.

Now the calendar has turned to December and I have become an illegal alien. We didn't tell the adjutant general about my tardy situation, afraid that ethically, he would be obligated to send me away or turn me in or something. I think I could have crossed a border and come back and been okay, but again, we can't afford a train ticket.

I belong nowhere. A criminal strolling down the street. I cannot enter military places without an escort, and in the case of Camp des Loges, without signing in and out. At the PX and commissary, even with an escort, I'm not allowed. I borrow other people's IDs to flash at these places when I really need to enter. I am surprised that this works. It must be a federal offense. Soldiers have a green ID and dependents have an orange ID. Few women in the 1960s populated the military. Flashing a green ID card with a man's picture, many times a black man's picture, seems like a fast way to prison. Not just for me, but the guy doing the lending.

The trip to the PX when we buy our wedding rings mandates my participation. The PX has no federal tax on jewelry. The rings we purchase are marked $25, costing $12.50 each. They are quarter-inch wide gold bands. I love them. After almost forty years my ring looks as good as Al's, and his has spent most of those years in a jewelry box while mine has been on my finger for that long. Why with money so tight did we buy him a ring?

We have finished the army tasks and thanks to the adjutant general we have notarized translations of the parent permission and the military papers required by the French government. Time to apply to the French government for permission to marry. In France, you don't get a marriage license as we know it in the United States. You make arrangements with the local *mairie* ("mayor's office") in the *hotel de ville* ("city hall"), to be married by the mayor of the village. After you have an official marriage at the mayor's office, you may have any religious service you wish. So off I go to the mayor's office in Boulogne-Billancourt.

Remember Boulogne-Billancourt, the city in which we live, next to the city of Paris? Boulogne-Billancourt where all the electricity is 220 volts, not 110 volts like we have in the United States. Some parts of Paris use

110, and most hotels also have 110. We have to be careful in buying light bulbs, and we have to use a transformer to run any appliances.

Al's Aunt gave me an electric skillet for a wedding present before I left and his mom suggested that I ship it, as I did not know what kind of stove I would have. The transformer is big and awkward and noisy so I don't like to use it. The PX sold some appliances that would run on 220 so after saving up of course, we bought a 220 radio and a 220 toaster.

Al had purchased an old record player from a GI returning stateside. When we moved into the apartment, we plugged it in and it blew up. Al fixed it after a trip to the PX for parts.

The radio is wonderful. We have Armed Forces Network, which has old-time radio show like *Our Miss Brooks* and *Jack Benny*. After we bought the radio, I changed the furniture arrangement. I put the bed up against the west wall, which then covered an electrical outlet. French outlets are just two little round holes in the wall. They don't have the concave entrance like U.S. outlets, which helps when trying to make a connection when you can't see the outlet. After moving the bed I try to plug in a lamp. I can feel the outlet but keep missing it with the plug. I finally put my index finger of my right hand across the two prongs of the plug. With my left hand I felt for the outlet. I knew when I made the connection because the shock from the 220 volts threw me up into the air and onto my back on the bed. I lay there with my heart pounding and my fillings dancing in my mouth for about ten minutes. I finally stagger to the phone and call Al. I explain what happened and ask him what to do for the shock. He replies, "If you are talking to me, you are fine."

Al received a promotion in rank in October or November. A promotion comes with more money, but we are still poor. When we marry we will get dependent pay. Not married, the two of us are living on a paycheck meant for one.

Another place we get money every three months is from a United

States savings bond. The company commander wants everyone in the company to participate in the "voluntary" savings bond program. The smallest amount that can be taken from a paycheck is one-third of a $25 bond. So every three months we are issued a $25 savings bond, which is worth $12.50, and as soon as we get it we cash it. The bank that cashes it takes a fee, so thanks to the company commander, we lose money we really need. That practice has left me bitter about participating in savings bond programs ever since. I refuse to participate to this day even though my current employer tries to be as persuasive as the company commander.

Our banking practices are pretty simple. Al gets paid the first of each month. He cashes his check and changes enough dollars into francs to pay rent, phone, gas, and electricity, buy metro tickets and movie tickets. We keep our money under the shelf paper on the middle shelf of the armoire. We use U.S. currency in the PX, commissary, and snack bar. To supplement the PX we have a Montgomery Ward's catalog. We can buy things from the catalog and they ship to our APO address. At the PX we buy money orders to send with our catalog order since we have no credit cards or checking account.

The spiffy new 1963 Christmas toy catalogue has a slot car set-up. This is a track somewhat like a toy train track but wider. Two cars could run side by side on the track and race. Each car has a control used to speed-up the cars for the straitaways or slow them down for the curves. Al selected the ones he wanted from the Montgomery Ward Christmas catalog. The slot-car set arrives in time for me to wrap it and place it under the Christmas tree. Al wants to play with it, but I say he has to wait for Christmas. Of course he knows what it is because he had to get the money order, and he was the only one who could pick up the APO mail.

It is only fair that I made him wait because he made sure I was completely surprised with the Christmas present he got for me. He knew I was a present snooper, so he bought my present just before Christmas. When he had to go to work he pulled a hair from my head, put the package in a high cupboard in the bathroom, and taped the hair over the door so it would break if the door is opened. He found this trick while reading James Bond 007 books. I got the stool from the kitchen and looked closely at the trap. I am sure I will be caught if I try to peek. I leave my surprise of a beautiful bracelet-watch for Christmas morning.

We ask our families for board games. So after Christmas Al teaches me to play chess with the set we received. We also like to play Chinese checkers. We keep a Monopoly game going for days, with the board on the floor and we walk around it.

We bought a Christmas tree in our neighborhood. They are for sale right on the street we take to and from the metro. From the PX we get a stand, lights, ornaments, and tinsel. It is a nice tree and it makes our little room festive. To have the lights on, though, we have to run the noisy transformer. The slot cars also need the transformer, but they are kind of noisy by themselves.

The Evil Woman

Across the street from the Marbeuf building is a café called Elysees Marbeuf, because it is on Avenue Marbeuf close to the Champs Elsees. As a result of its being across the street from the Marbeuf building and the owner being accommodating to GIs, even loaning money or carrying a tab at the end of the month, this is our hangout place.

In this place the guys getting off work at 8:00 A.M. could go and have a beer or two before going home, and no one thought badly of them because we all functioned under different schedules.

I learn to eat snails (escargot) at Elysees Marbeuf. They are on the menu as a sort of snack, and not at all expensive or pretentious.

In the winter, cafes will have a stall facing the street, or you might encounter a cart on the street with oysters. These also sell at a very reasonable cost. Squeeze a little lemon on the raw oyster and toss it in your mouth, oh my, a tasty treat. It is said if you do this with your companion under the stars you will have a night filled with romance.

When my mother learned I had developed a taste for these items she couldn't believe it, as I was her picky-eater child.

My biggest regret of opportunities missed, is trying horse meat. There are almost as many horse butchers as beef butchers, but we shop only in the commissary. A whole carcass of beef hangs right at the butcher's door so you pass close to it as you walk down the street. Just walking from my apartment to the metro is an olfactory adventure. Butcher shops have a subtle odor enhanced by the temperature of the day, and most memorable is in summer. Poultry shops are enclosed so their smells don't linger, but the sight of chickens and ducks without feathers but still retaining their heads and feet will cause me to stop and look at their bumpy complexion and blank gaze. They lie in un-refrigerated windows, tempting shoppers who find them attractive. I just find them curious. If they stay in the window too long the skin dries and wrinkles and does not look like dinner to me. Cheese shops, and of course, the fish market give off the most pungent odors. My second regret is that my taste for cheese develops too late in life to reward myself with a different cheese each day of the year as I live and breathe the Paris charm.

The smell, which I hated then but brings Paris most to mind now is the strong tobacco scent of the French cigarette Gitanes. Paris also comes to mind when I am walking on an overcast day and a truck or a tractor puts a hint of diesel exhaust fumes in the air. A lot of European cars are diesel, and a damp day would fill the air with that vapor.

New Year's Eve is grand fun. We have a high school friend who is in the army stationed in Germany visiting us. Al has to be at work at midnight on New Year's Eve so we all go into town after dinner – Al, our friend Todd, and me.

We go to Elysees Marbeuf to visit with our friends and have a New Year's drink. About 11:00 P.M. or I should say, about 2300, we leave Elysees Marbeuf to stroll up the Champs Elysees and over to the BlockHouse so Al can go to work. However, the entire Champs Elysees is a party. Foot travelers greeting auto occupants with a kiss or drink or a *bon annee*. A ten-minute walk took us almost two hours.

Todd and I leave Al at the BlockHouse and return to Elysees Marbeuf.

Todd is drinking with his fellow soldiers and when I go downstairs to go to the bathroom, I find a ten-year-old boy who has accompanied his parents to a private party in the basement of Elysees Marbeuf. The boy and I keep each other company. He knows no English. His mother knows a little English. She is sitting on the corner of a large table of partygoers and when needed, the boy and I go to her for a translation. The boy keeps talking to me as we entertain each other upstairs and down. I keep saying to him, "*Je ne parle pas Français*" (I do not speak French), and because I say it in French, it must not make any sense to him because he keeps talking to me. After a while his mother makes a bed for him in the corner and I return to Todd and our other friends.

The metro closes at 2:00 A.M. so we have to celebrate until the first metro at 5:00 A.M. We are not the only ones. A crowd of people slowly forms at to top of the stairs of the Franklin D. Roosevelt stop. It is a very pleasant evening, night, or morning, weather-wise.

Many French people go to costume parties for New Year's, so our metro car has several wild-looking characters. There is a lot of joking and laughing going on. Quite the contrast to the solemn, un-smiling people I usually encounter riding the metro. One man is dressed as a woman and reaches inside his bra and pulls out an apple that was being used to create a breast. He takes a bite of the apple and returns it to the bra. This causes all sorts of laughs and jokes, and more laughs. I wish I could understand all the jokes. I enjoy the visual jokes and laugh along with everyone else. What a fun trip home.

Holidays are over and time to get back to work.

I talk to a clerk at the Boulogne-Billancourt mayor's office about arranging my marriage. She explains I need a *carte de sejour* from the *Prefecture de Police*. Oh great! Now the criminal must to go the France's main police building.

Using the word "explain" makes the process sound too simple. Clerks working in the mayor's office in Boulogne-Billancourt do not encounter foreigners often. They may have had some English in school, but not much. The one helping me probably learned, "The pen is on the table." "*Le crayon est sur la table.*" All I can remember from French class is, "*A la bibliotheque, vite.*" "To the library, quick." If we could go to the library we could get a French/English dictionary and point at some words for each other. We might find some comprehension. She has a conversation with her colleagues, none of whom can find the words to explain to me what I need, so she writes on a piece of paper: "carte de sejour" and "Prefecture de Police."

A carte de sejour is a card of residence. Like a green card in the United States. Al doesn't need one because he is military, but until the moment we both say, "I do," I need the permission from the French government to live here. French law also requires a ninety-day residency to get married. Without a carte de sejour, I am not a resident. I am only a visitor and must I say it again, a visitor who has overstayed her welcome.

Al and I locate the Prefecture de Police on the metro map and one day while he works, I take my note to do my French task. I ride the metro to stop Cite. As I leave the train I see an exit at either end of the platform. I follow the crowd to the more popular exit and find myself on a shopping street. I walk up and down and up and down, not finding anything that resembles a government building or police station or where I need to go.

I finally go into a small dress shop. Inside I find three delightful women. I show my note. One woman begins talking and pointing and I look out the window in the direction she is pointing and looked back at her, as I have no idea what she is telling me. She and the other women have a discussion and each tries to give me directions. They each speak slowly and carefully, but I am still the ignorant country bumpkin living some place where I do not know the language. Finally, one woman put both her arms straight out, then bends them at the elbows and lays her right forearm over her left forearm, then picking up her right arm and using two fingers like little legs, walks along her left forearm.

Oh! I exclaim across the bridge! Smiles and laughs all around, I say, "*Merci beaucoup*," and off I go. Now, I realize that when I got off the metro train and gone to the other exit I would have come up on the other side of the river and been right at the door of the Prefecture.

The Prefecture de Police is an old, dark building with tall, heavy huge doors. The door squeaks open and I squeeze in. The *thud* behind me as the door let itself fall shut echoes off the high ceiling. This is a scary place even if I weren't a criminal. I soon encounter a uniformed gendarme exhibit my note and he directs me up the stairs. The stairs must be ten feet wide and each step dips from wear of centuries. The first flight of stairs leads only to a large landing. There is a huge window on the landing wall ten feet up and twenty feet tall. But the cloudy Paris sky gives only an eerie glow. I turn and mount the second flight of stairs. I wander down the hall to the place where I hear voices and find a pleasant woman to whom I reveal my note. This woman knows a little English and she takes me to the office of another woman who turns out to be evil, in my opinion. I present the evil woman my note. The evil woman is sitting behind a large desk; she looks up at me with a glare and in a voice of disgust gives me several sentences of information. Then she looks back down at the paper work on her desk. As far as she is concerned, I have disappeared. I take a step toward her and softly say, "I'm sorry I do not understand." She rolls her eyes up without moving her head, speaks rudely and returns to her work. Now I start to get upset and a little too loudly I say, "I DON'T UNDERSTAND YOU." She never flinched. There is no way she is going to pay any attention to me. I leave her office and find the nice woman again. Now I am trying to control my tears. The nice woman and the evil woman have words. The nice woman tells me I must return with my fiancée.

This sortie to the Prefecture has taken place on a Friday. Al is working days. Days of the week mean nothing to his schedule of six days working and two days off. Saturday is just another workday to him. So we arrange to meet at the Prefecture at 11:30 A.M., during Al's lunch on Saturday. He gets held up at work and is a little late. When he arrives we find our way back to the evil woman's office and find the door shut and a line of couples outside the door. We hope it doesn't take too long, as Al has to get back to work. We take our place in line. The door opens a slit. A couple comes out, a couple goes in. We wait. All the couples seem to be about our age. One part of each couple must not be a citizen of France. Everyone is solemn, with long faces. I am thinking that like me, they have all met this evil woman before. Door opens, couple in, couple out. We wait. One couple ahead of us, the door opens. The evil woman, holding the door, lets her head and arm enter the hall. Then wagging her finger as only the French can do, she says, "*Fini, fini, fini.*" It is 12:30; her Saturday workday is done.

I am frozen in place. My stomach knots up, my chin begins to quiver, and I feel the pain behind my eyes from the ocean of tears I am holding back. It is not considered polite to be emotional in public in France. Al gently leads me away and we take the metro to Marbeuf to have lunch. One of Al's work friends joins us at our table and casually asks, "So, how's it goin' for you guys to get married?" And the flood breaks lose and the ocean flows from my eyes.

Monday evening, after Al gets off work, finds us back at the Prefecture. It is January and after 5:00 P.M.; it is dark already. Now the place looks and feels even more sinister. We go into the evil woman's office. She asks to see Al's military ID. Since my reason for being in the country is to marry my American military boyfriend, I guess producing said boyfriend is proof enough. She gives us a paper and directs us back to the area where I found the agreeable woman. She acts as matter-of-fact as can be. I don't know what directives adorn this document. It must give approval for me to stay in France until I get married. But then, the evil woman doesn't know my visa has expired.

We venture down the hall. In this large room, situated along the far wall are several extended tables placed end-to-end, with bureaucrats on one side and aliens on the other. When a space opens up, we take a seat on the alien side, with our aristocrat across. We give her our paper from the evil woman. She asks for my passport. I hand it over. She throws herself back. Her eyes open wide. She exclaims, "*Oh la la.*" Al half stands. removes his wallet from his back pocket takes out one hundred francs (twenty dollars) and hands it to her. She takes the franc note and my passport and scurries down along the wall and disappears. I am confused. I didn't hear her ask for money. I turn to Al to ask what is going on and he hushes me. We sit and wait. We have no idea what will happen next. I expect her to return with gendarmes to take me to jail. She reappears, and her behavior is very business-like. She hands me my passport, which now contains a new stamp under the stamp I received on my arrival, and a paper for the Mairie de Boulogne-Billancourt. We are done, not "done for." We exhale and rise slowly from our chairs.

No change came back from the hundred francs. The stamp in my passport says: "*Taxe percue* 40F" (duty collected, forty francs). I add bribing an official to my list of offenses. I hope the worst part is over. The stamp does not say *carte de sejour* either. It says, "*Prefecture de Police direction de la police generale Recu No 5469 Fait a Paris 27 JANV 1964.*" The best I can figure, this stamp gives me an exemption, number 5469, until the 27th of January to get my business done. So I guess I'll be married by the end of January, or I should say, I had better be married by the end of January.

I take my new stamp and all the papers back to the mayor's office in Boulogne-Billancourt. They give me two forms, one form for the best man and the other for the maid of honor. These forms are to verify that the witnesses are of sound mind and old enough to be witnesses. When the forms are completed and signed, I return them. Ray will be the best man. The maid of honor will be my friend Janine.

I met Janine when I first arrived. She is a "valley girl." In 1963 it is two decades before valley girl means blond, blue-eyed girl raised with all the luxury found under the pleasant southern California sun. She isn't a valley girl with a "like you know, gag me" speech pattern. In fact, her favorite word is "amazing." She never complains or criticizes. So "amazing" works well because she is always describing something delightful.

She attended Catholic school for eight years, so you know the nuns taught her to speak quite well. She attended Hollywood High, which she found "amazingly" fun, and she graduated in 1961. She went to school with stars; kids who would become stars and children of stars. She worked a short time as a long-distance operator for the phone company. Back then there was only one phone company. She had interesting stories to tell about placing calls for stars. She can be as starstruck as the rest of us even though she and her siblings all had small parts in movies as children. Her close encounters with the famous sounds exciting, but I believe her luckiest lot in life is her fascinating family.

Janine's grandfather (an American) made a million selling motorcycles to Japan. Then, with all good timing, made another million buying motorcycles from Japan. While living in Japan his daughter (Janine's mother), fell in love with a French man (Janine's father). I don't know what Janine's father was doing in Japan. These two people got married and lived in France until they escaped from the Nazis and then lived happily in Southern California for many years. Her father's family business required that he return to France in 1962. Janine lives with her family in France, and she meets many Americans in the USO (United Services Organization) in Paris. I meet Janine at the snack bar. We become friends and she is to be my maid of honor.

Janine works in an office that provides financing and insurance for GIs purchasing a car. She is dating Robert, an army guy from Southern California. They met in Paris, not California. The four of us spend a lot of time together.

I take the witness forms, have them properly filled out by Ray and Janine, and return them to the mayor's office. It is really close now. I think we will be married soon.

The Concierge

In the United States, the basis of our civil law was established by the founding fathers. In France, the Catholic Church, the Monarchs, Napoleon, and their own revolution all had a hand in establishing civil law, which brings us back to the subject of marriage banns. I took the witness forms back to the Mairie de Boulogne-Billancourt and found that the French require the banns of marriage be posted outside the mayor's office for three weeks. An obvious carryover of church law into civil law. Now who do you think stops by the mayor's office around the side of the facility to view the banns of marriage? Well, I do.

Hanging on the side of the building in a little cupboard with locked glass doors are all the public notices for the village. I locate the line with our names and address. It is exciting to see it there. I'm tickled. I'm getting married soon! Other people also stopped to look at these names and addresses. Some of these people are florists, wedding dress shop owners, tuxedo shop owners, and any merchant connected to weddings. I know this because they all begin to send us advertisements in the mail.

Apartment buildings in France have an apartment on the ground floor near the front door for the concierge. The concierge is responsible for cleaning the stairs and corridors, delivering the mail for the building to each apartment, monitoring other deliveries, and generally watching who comes and goes. We have never gotten mail at our apartment. All our letters and packages are delivered to Al at the BlockHouse. Our APO (Army Post Office) directs our correspondence there.

The 1960s will become known as the decade of decadence, but I have never heard of anyone living together before getting married. I did not want the concierge to know that Al and I are not married. I want to wear my wedding ring after its purchase. Al thinks it will be nicer if we wait until we are married. So I wear my high school class ring on my left hand and turn it around to look like a band each time I see the concierge.

Now we are getting mail with little brides and grooms on the envelopes shoved under our door by the concierge. I think I will die. Al asks what I am upset about and I say, "Now the concierge knows we are not married." He replies, "So what?" And I guess he is correct because soon after we did it, living together before marriage became the norm.

The kitchen window gives me an opportunity for another encounter with the concierge. The window, with thick rumpled glass, let in the light, but obstructed sight. Each of the six panes is about fifteen by twenty inches. Twisting the knob in the middle of the window causes it to unlatch, and the two sides swing in. Just as I start to pull, a tight spot requires an extra tug on the left side. The putty around some of the panes has dried and loosened and come out in places. When I tug at the tight spot, the panes rattle. One of the panes is quite wobbly so I fix it by placing some tape where the putty is missing.

I try to keep the same hours as Al while he works different shifts. When I don't do this successfully, I end up sitting on the floor of the bathroom reading while Al sleeps, so I don't bother him. Keeping these hours causes me to be doing housework late at night on some shifts.

A multi-level apartment allows sounds from above to broadcast below. One evening, kind of late, while doing housework, I hear a knock on the door. I am surprised. No one ever comes to our door. The woman standing there spoke to me in French and made hand gestures indicating I am noisy and that she is trying to sleep. Following that, I try to keep my activities low after 9:00 P.M. Late one warm summer night, not a creature was stirring, not even a mouse. I am tiptoeing around finishing my work. Just before I go to bed I close the kitchen window. I give an extra push at the tight spot. The putty and the tape both fail. A single pane of glass sails out as silently as a feather floats. I freeze on the spot. No motion, no sound, wait, wait, *CRASH!* I hear the famous "*Oh la la*" of a female voice lacerate the silent night air. I don't move for at least five minutes, and then quiet as I can, I crawl into bed.

Next morning I ring the concierge bell and motion for her to come with me. She follows me to my apartment and I show her the window. She indicates she wants writing material, and I give her paper and pencil. She writes on the paper a name and telephone number. I call my friend Janine and ask her to call and make an appointment for me to have my window fixed. I tell her the phone number and then I spell the name v-i-t-r-i-e-r. She just starts laughing, and I can't figure out why. What has the concierge written? When Janine settles down she explains to me his name is not Vitrier. He IS a *vitrier*. A *vitrier* works with glass, or glazier in English.

Janine makes the call for me. The *vitrier* arrives right on time and does a wonderful job fixing my window. He cleans up after himself really well. The nicest service man I have ever seen. When he finishes he presents his bill and I look at the amount and pay him that sum. He is very polite. Says, "*Merci, au revoir*," and leaves. I am unaware I have just committed the most conspicuous faux pas.

I call Janine to tell her how nice the guy was and what a good job he did. She asks, "Did you tip him?" I tell her, "No, I didn't need to, he gave me a bill and I paid it." She explains the bill is just for materials. I feel so bad. Americans earn the adjective ugly by this kind of ignorance.

Another activity that must bother my neighbors is my doing laundry.

Each one of my four bathroom fixtures has its own sound when it collects water. I know this from hearing my own and from listening to the clatter, clank, rattle, and rumble from the floor above. The toilet has the typical French *GAA-rush-ss*, the sink *spish*, the bidet *whoo-sha*, and the bathtub *ca-spash*. To do laundry, I put the clothes in the bathtub with soap and water. I try to mimic a washing machine by sloshing everything around with a mop handle. I ring them out from the tub to the bidet. Rinse them in the bidet and ring them out and place them in the sink for a second rinse. Ring them out at the sink, where standing I can ring harder, for hanging on the line over the tub. This process caused me to run water in the tub, then in the bidet, then in the sink, and repeat again. This must sound odd to the neighbors below.

In the spring of 1964 the army built a laundromat at bel manoir, which made the process better than doing it by hand in the three fixtures, but not much. I really like the laundromat mostly because of the dryers. Clothes hanging over the tub in damp Paris could take several days to dry. Going to the laundromat, I pack all the dirty clothes into the two large suitcases, which accompanied my arrival in Paris. I waddle down to the bus stop like I am going on an extended holiday. I lug my load onto the bus, ride to bel manoir, and haul my cargo off the bus. At bel manoir I do laundry, fold clean clothes into suitcases, and repeat the trip in reverse.

Before the army laundromat at bel manoir was built, I found a French laundromat run by an American. It is located several metro stops away with one train change, so the suitcases are a problem going there as well. At this laundromat the owner installed a token machine in which you deposit three 1-franc coins (sixty cents) and it gives you a token the size of a dime. This token operates the washers and dryers that the owner imported from the United States. That is why they work for a dime. Enterprising Americans simply use real dimes. This makes the owner quite angry. Not only is he losing fifty cents a load, it is difficult to change foreign coins. I am not the only American participating in this misdeed.

L'Oreal

After all we have been through, now we must wait three more weeks for the posting of the banns. I am not anxious while the banns make their declaration. In fact, I have a wonderful time. I go to school.

The main office of L'Oreal, the hair care company, is in Paris. I inquire there and they have a free two-week long school for foreign students. The reason the school is free is because if a hairdresser is familiar with using L'Oreal products, then the hairdresser is more likely to apply L'Oreal products in their salons. In my class I meet two young women from Sweden who speak English well, and we have a grand time together. A man from South Africa, a man and a woman each from a different place in the Middle East, and someone from Spain are also taking the class. Eight or ten of us from various worldwide locations make up the class. Each morning women wanting their hair colored or permed come to L'Oreal. The instructors examine the customers and explain to the students the process to follow. Once each student is paired with a customer, the students perform the required procedure.

Two instructors work with us. One speaks French and English and the other speaks French and Spanish. There is a student from Italy who has trouble with all three languages spoken by the instructors. I remember because one of my Swedish friends speaks Swedish, English, and Italian. She listens to the English instructions and translates them into Italian. There are several second – and third-hand translations going on while the instructor talks. I don't know how anyone gets her hair done correctly. In the afternoon we work on each other and attend a lecture. I remember the lecture hall but I cannot recall the language used for the presentations. I don't know if I just sat quietly or if I was possibly beginning to comprehend a bit of French or were the lectures somehow translated.

Afternoons when we work on each other we hang out in the room with all the hair dryers. These are casual, comfortable times and the most fun is doing tongue twisters in all the languages. Someone tells you a tongue twister in a language not your own. They say it several times, and then you say it back to them. You are not really saying the words, you are just repeating the sounds you hear. The errors you make in their language can be quite amusing. You don't know why they are laughing, but the laughter is infectious.

In 1982 Al and I returned to France for a visit with our then fourteen-year-old daughter. We showed her where we lived and where we were married, and I took her to L'Oreal. I explained to the receptionist that I had been a student there in 1964 and she took us both in front of the other women waiting, to have our hair permed. I heard a woman protest about being there before us and the receptionist replied something about we were special.

I will always have very fond memoirs of L'Oreal.

The two Swedish girls and I go to lunch together every day. One rainy day while running across the street, one of the girls steps in a puddle and says, "Oh hell." When seated in the restaurant, I ask her, "You learned your English in school, right?" She says, "Yes," so I say, "Did they teach you, oh hell?" "Oh," she cries, putting her hand to her mouth. "Is that a very bad thing to say?" I tell her it's not and explain what it means. She says she likes to go to American movies and listen to the dialog and imitate the speech.

The Swedish girls are on a budget as tight as mine. They are both seventeen or eighteen, and their parents have sent them to Paris for just the two weeks of the school. They have a cheap hotel without a bath or shower. So the Sunday between the two weeks' classes they come over to our apartment to bathe. Al is working day shift, so the three of us just hang out doing girl stuff. The bathing went well, but we ran out of hot water. While they are at our place they drink all our milk. They said it is like Swedish milk, and that they are really missing some good milk because they can't find that kind in France. I don't know where the army gets the milk it sells in the commissary and convenience store, but it is processed the American way, and I guess, the Swedish way as well. I truly enjoy the company of two friends my age. Fresh, new friends not at all connected to the military. It is a fabulous two weeks and when the Swedish girls leave, we swear to keep in touch, but never did. This is a big regret of mine.

I am beginning to pick up a little French, but not enough. Once I left our apartment late and didn't have a watch. As I hurry to the metro, I want to know the time. I see a woman standing in a doorway so I approach her and say, "*Quelle heure est-il?*" She looks at her watch and says, "*Blah blah blah, blah blah blah blah.*" I smile, say, "*Merci,*" and move on. How stupid! I know enough French to ask, "What time is it?" but not enough to understand the answer. Ever since that day, whenever anyone asks me the time and most especially if they have an accent, I show them my watch so they can read the time themselves.

My feelings of inadequacy are made even worse when I am with our friends, Horace and Christina. Horace and Al met on the way to France aboard a military ship. Since Al left home courtesy of his father's gift ticket, he had hardly a dime in his pocket. By the time he reached France, he had nothing. Horace, very tall and a few years older, took Al under his wing and helped him out until payday. Horace does the same maintenance work that Al does so he and Al are always on different shifts. Horace is dating Christina. Christina is from Sweden and works in the Swedish Embassy in Paris. My two friends from L'Oreal had some business with their embassy, and because I know Christina, I know where to take them.

When Al is working, Horace and Christina entertain me with movies and visiting cafés on the left bank. Once, when we are looking for a certain movie theater, Christina asks directions from a man standing on a corner. She asks in French. When the man said he did not speak French, Christina asks what he spoke, and finding the man prefers German, Christina asks directions in German. I am in awe of Christina.

Married in Boulogne-Billancourt

After the three-week wait for the banns, I return to the *Mairie de Boulogne-Billancourt* and lo and behold, the only question they have is, "What day would you like to get married?" It is Monday, February 3; I have passed my January 27 deadline given to me by the Prefecture of Police to wrap up my business. Still, I consider giving myself some time to get ready. How much more ready do I have to be? I think of making the date a week from Saturday, but when I look at the calendar, Wednesday after next is Ash Wednesday, the first day of Lent. Catholics can get married during Lent, but it is not a good idea so, Saturday, February 8, 1964 becomes the date.

Al is working afternoon shift the week of the wedding. He goes into Paris early on Thursday to the American Catholic Church to attend confession. This is the same church where we went for the Kennedy mass. After Al leaves, I dig out my wedding dress. This dress has been hanging in the back of the tiny little closet for five months. I discover the coal-burning furnaces and damp Paris air have turned the dress from glossy white to dirty yellow.

I hang the dress up and look at it from across the room. It cannot be worn the way it looks. There are no care instructions on the garment. I don't even know the kind of material. I look it over to see if I can find a place to do a test cleaning. I decide to sacrifice the over-skirt by washing it in the sink, and if it turns out badly, I will just wear the yellow dress. Overwhelmed with the stress of the moment, I plunged the over-skirt into the sink filled with soapy water. I swish it around; it didn't shrivel up or fall apart. I take it out; it doesn't look too bad but it is still wet. I rinse it well and hang it up. I can't believe it, when it dries, it is as good as new! I wash the whole dress in the sink and everything turns out delightful! All I have to do is a little touch-up ironing on the dress lining.

I go to confession on Friday. I get the priest with the British accent and no teeth. He is very hard to understand. I confess to him that Al and I are living together; he tells me I must leave the apartment until after the wedding. I tell him that I have nowhere to go. I explain to him that if Al were to leave he could stay with a work friend, but the priest insists, I must leave.

One of the guys, with whom Al works, re-enlisted on the first of December. He uses his re-enlistment bonus to go home to Pennsylvania over Christmas and get married and bring his bride back. What a good idea! They decided to get married after my arrival in Paris and they are married before we are. Al is not ready to sell three more years of his life for plane tickets. This couple now lives across the street from us. Their apartment has two rooms and nice furniture. They pay more in rent than we pay. They live there just a couple of months then move to a cheaper place on the north side of Paris. When Al got off work Friday night he went to their place trying to satisfy the priest's wishes. To all my crimes, I now add sins. The three of them, still up at 2:00 A.M. celebrating our big day call me to come over and join them. It is 4:00 or 5:00 A.M. before we stagger home.

I asked Janine to get a corsage for herself and a bouquet for me. She did a wonderful job. My bouquet is beautiful. I gave up on any idea of having a cake.

Al asked Stamer to work for him Saturday. There are five guys including Al who do the same job. Four of them do the rotating shifts and Stamer, the most senior, works only day shift on weekdays. He is not a close friend to our bunch, and many times, he is the subject of ridicule for his strange ways. When Al asked Stamer to cover for him, Stamer refuses as he thinks Al is too young to get married and that he is attempting to save him from trouble. Yes, Stamer was very much aware of our tribulations to reach this point. He still felt he was doing Al a favor by not working for him. Or maybe he really is just a butthead. One of the other guys filled in for Al.

We ask Delbert Speed to drive us all to the mayor's office and then to Camp de Loges because he has a big car. His car is a four-door, with bench seats front and back. It holds six people. Speed is a genuine pleasing guy with a James Dean smile. He wears sunglasses day and night in this city with no sun. He is quiet yet attentive. When anyone asks him where he is from he smiles and says, "Paris." He gets odd looks and comments, but it is the truth; he is from Paris, Texas. Lots of the guys smoke unfiltered Pall-Malls and tap each cigarette before lighting it to pack the tobacco. Speed smokes filter cigarettes but he always removes one from the pack and his Zippo lighter from his pocket and taps the cigarette on the side of the lighter heartily for a lengthy duration. I don't recall him smoking, just tapping. Maybe he doesn't have a smoking habit, just a tapping habit.

With only five days notice we invite everyone to the wedding by word of mouth. Many of the guys would be training at Camp de Loges on Saturday morning so we asked them to come over to the chapel after training.

While the banns were posted I wish I had gone to the mayor's office on a Saturday morning to see how this French wedding thing is done. I didn't know the French women wear their wedding gowns to the Mairie, and then to the church.

Without this knowledge, I wear a nice suit to the Mairie and then when we get to Camp de Loges I have to change into my wedding dress. The chapel at Camp de Loges is very small, with no place for me to change. Janine and I go next door, to an empty lunchroom and while I change, some guys pass the window and get quite an eyeful. Janine is so cute. She tells me that it doesn't count on your wedding day. I am so confused I believe her.

My wedding dress is beautiful in spite of, or because of, its recent encounter with detergent.

We have looked forward to this day for so long that when Speed and Janine arrive at our place Al won't wake up. He had lain down with his clothes on when we got home from across the street. Now he is sound asleep. Janine wants to make him some coffee. I tell her go to the kitchen and get him a Coke. This amuses her; I thought she knew us better than that. We have been living on Coke and cigarettes. We get Al up and dressed. Then Ray, the best man, calls to ask how he is to get to our place. He knows the time we all have to be at the mayor's office. Evidently, he and Al didn't talk about his transportation. Janine asked Speed to pick her up, but Ray had not. When Ray calls, it is too late for him come to our place and then go with us to the mayor's office. We tell him to take the metro to the Billancourt stop and meet us at the mayor's office. I know this could mean trouble when I tell him this. The mayor's office is located close to the Billancourt stop, but you can't see the building when you come up to the sidewalk from the metro. You go straight a few steps then turn right for about half a block, then the street of the mayor's office joins the street you are on at an angle across the street on your left. This is a zigzag tricky route, but not that uncommon for the wacky streets of Paris. If you don't get started down the right street when you get off the metro, you can get really lost. I knew this, and Ray is about to find this out, to all our sorrow.

I now feel the same way I felt the day I got on the airplane. Plans made and I know what I need to do, but stress and lack of sleep add to the calamity of the morning.

We get to the mayor's office and go into the big room for weddings.

It has massive windows covered with long shear drapes and about ten rows of pews with a center aisle. The doors to this room have been closed on my other visits. I'm happy with this impressive place. In front, a twenty-by-three-foot dais sits on a raised platform. In the middle and behind the dais, there is a large chair facing the pews. On the right side of the dais a very large book. I mean a huge book. The book rests on a stand that tips it forward. It lies open. It must be two feet tall and fifteen inches thick. Another article on the dais is a shallow basket. Janine makes sure we have money to place in the basket, as a tip to the mayor.

The time to start approaches, and there is no Ray. We get Speed to take off his sunglasses. We explain to him that we already handed in papers with Ray's name as the witness. So Speed starts repeating Raymond Windorff under his breath so he will remember to answer to Ray's name. My head spinning, I think, *Is this it. Am I being married today.*

Five months since I left my mother's side, and in that time, I have trespassed on government facilities, used false documents to enter government property, lived in a country without proper documentation, cheated a washing machine, and bribed an official. Now I am a conspirator in fraud and forgery. I stayed in my house last night to iron my dress, and that act became a sin. September 7, 1963, the beginning of a slide down the slippery slope to a life of degradation.

There are about half a dozen other weddings scheduled for today. The other wedding parties include family and friends. All the other brides wear long, beautiful wedding gowns. Janine explains that each couple will be married individually. We should go to the front when the mayor calls our name. We should say, "*Oui,*" when the mayor looks at us.

The mayor gets everyone's attention, and the room goes quiet. Standing in front of the dais he says a few words and calls the first couple, second, third, then us. It is fortunate we are not first. We get to see how it is done before we are called. We must look odd to all the others. Just the four of us, no wedding gown, and Al in his uniform.

The mayor does well pronouncing our non-French names. The four of us go to the front. I find it difficult to remember all that happened because I understand little of what was said, and we all worry that Speed will slip up in answering to and signing Ray's name. Each time it is Speed's turn, we hold our breath. His slow, Texas rhythm produces a pause then, "*Oui.*" The rest of us manage our "*ouis*" at about the right time. Then in turn, the four of us sign the big book and several other papers. Inside, my head screams, *Please Speed, sign Windorff.* We are finished! We take our seats. Now, waiting for the others is strenuous. What if Ray comes barging in after Speed has done the exploit? I want to find Ray and be on our way to the chapel.

After everyone finishes we leave the building and look around for Ray. We take some pictures on the steps, look for Ray, and then race to Camp de Loges. Al considers it a proper wedding day because we travel over one hundred miles per hour to get to the church on time.

No one has heard from, or knows the whereabouts of Ray. Not a Catholic, Speed returns to the roll of chaffer. Janine's boyfriend, Robert, Catholic and wearing his uniform, becomes the best man at the church. Janine and I find the lunchroom for me to change. The altar boy's mother and sister would be the only mass attendees, if it were not for us. They look on with surprise and fascination at our vivacity. The priest is getting impatient to start.

At the chapel, Bob and Fey, the couple from across the street, Montgomery, Amey, and a new kid named Dale Mackey wait for the show to begin. Anyone who joins the group after you is new. Mackey is a big boy, six feet tall, and hefty. I think of him as a kid; he is seventeen or eighteen and I am all of nineteen. Anyway, he is in uniform because he had been at training that morning. The other guys are in suits. I grab Mackey's arm and tell him that he is going to walk me down the aisle.

Al and Robert stand in the front of the church. Our few guests and the altar boy's family are all seated in the pews. Janine goes down the aisle; Mackey and I walk down the aisle. I wish more people had come to fill the chapel because all of a sudden, I really miss my family. I would give anything if my mother and sisters could be here for my wedding.

We stand before the priest. I hear Al repeating he will love and honor me. I look into his face and I am filled with peace and joy. We have a very quick wedding and a mass. The priest doesn't even turn around to sprinkle the holy water; he half turns and gives it a fling. I push myself up a little from my kneeling position so a drop or two will fall on my head. This guy is in a hurry. In spite of everything, this is my one and only wedding, and I will forever have fond memories of it.

After mass, Al and I go to the back of the church for handshakes, hugs, and kisses. Al, having been an altar boy himself, slips the boy a little money for his extra work. We take some pictures in the chapel. When we exit the chapel we are showered with rice. I am thrilled our friends have remembered to do this.

Someone took a picture of Mackey and me going down the aisle. Mackey sent a copy of the picture to his parents with no explanation. I was told his parents wrote him a letter saying I looked like a very nice girl. They must have been pretty panicked, until they heard the whole story.

We add Amey, Robert, and Montgomery to Speed's car. Three guys in front, and the girls on laps in back. We stop at the PX at bel manor on our way back to Paris. Some of the people need to buy gifts before our reception tonight. I pretend not to notice. Do you think they waited until today to be sure we are really married? I guess that would be a good plan. Al and I wait in the car. Robert and Janine prepare lunch for us at Robert's apartment. Such a gracious gesture. Robert, excited to demonstrate his ability to deep-fry a whole chicken. The chicken, is quite memorable because of its rare condition; rare, as in not cooked well. Other than that, we enjoy a pleasant lunch and gracious toasts. I try to nap, but on this blessed day, my wedding day, sleep won't come. I put on a jacket of Robert's over my wedding dress and the four of us return to our apartment via the metro. Al carries me over the threshold several times for pictures from different cameras. The strain of this activity begins to show on his face in the last picture.

I do a quick clean up of the apartment. Janine insists on a picture of me in my wedding dress running the vacuum. I find it refreshing to have a vacuum and get the dirt out of the cracks in the floor. I borrowed the vacuum from Bob and Fey across the street. We also borrow chairs so our friends will have a place to sit. Our guests begin to arrive. Our guests are everyone we invited to the wedding. More people find it easier and more fun to attend a party close to Paris than a wedding way out at Camp de Loges. We have an extraordinary party.

Ray shows up with his dismal tale of being lost with no French money and no place to exchange money. He feels debased. He wondered what we were doing without him and sorry that he missed the wedding. We feel bad because he wasn't with us, and we didn't know what had happened to him. Gleefully, he made it to the party.

I have pictures of our guests sitting in our apartment holding little plates and drinks. For the life of me I cannot remember what we are eating and drinking. I don't even remember that we had enough dishes to feed guests. I have a picture of Ray wearing my lacy apron and helping do dishes. I guess the refreshments were a collaboration, and everyone brought something.

I stood half a flight up the stairs and threw my bouquet to the women standing by our door. The bouquet was caught by Speed's date. I do not know this nice-looking young woman. I don't think anything came of her catch.

Around midnight Janine starts trying to get everyone to leave so the bride and groom can be alone. I remind her that the evening shift has not yet arrived, but she persists. We bid good-bye, thank, kiss, and hug all our guests and find ourselves home alone on our wedding night. We picked up a bit and having nothing else to do, I change into the negligee I bought for this evening. I am doing a prancing waltz around the room when we hear the loud mufflers and screeching tires of the cars bringing the evening shift guys to the party. I jump back into my dress, and round two of the party is ready to roll.

So we had two parties to celebrate two ceremonies, but changing the witness, is it legal? Are we really married? We now have the paperwork that gets us dependent pay, so that is legal enough for us.

The Honeymoon

A few months after the wedding the army sent Al to a work-related school in Germany for six weeks. The school hides in a small army post in a tiny German village named Linggries, tucked into the foothills of the Alps. I take the train for a weekend visit, and I call this my honeymoon. Words fail me to describe the most enchanting weekend ever. We stay in the only Gasthaus in town. I don't know how many guestrooms it has; four or six, I speculate. Our room equals wonderful! It has a balcony facing the mountains; soft and cuddly down pillows and quilts induce the bed to snuggle you. You don't have to make an effort to snuggle into the bed.

After nine months of stumbling around learning the ways of the world and the ways of the French, I find myself traveling alone in a whole new country with a new language. I know what German phrases I need to function. "Coke please," "thank you," and "where is the bathroom?" On the train a young man comes through the cars selling candy and drinks. I stop him and say, "*Ein Coka bitte,*" and he says, "Five pfenigs, please." My accent is so strong he knows that he should respond in English.

In Munich, I change trains. I have trouble finding the train I need because it is not in the train station. It is behind the train station, on a narrow gauge track that goes up into the mountains. The cutest little train! This dated train has old-fashioned wooden seats. The time is late afternoon. I suspect this must be the commuter train used by the mountain villagers who work in Munich. All the cars are filled with people. I see guys in lederhosen with big bottles of beer. The bottles have the wire spring tops so they can be opened and closed. The lederhosen guys sit on the floor because all the seats are full. They toast each other and talk and laugh. I wish I could understand their jokes. They wear lederhosen as work clothes, not costumes. This is the real deal. The train, crammed with happy people, chugs up the mountain. Friday, the end of the workweek, adds to the high spirits.

The train *choo-choos* along and stops at every village. I sit quietly through a few stops. All the people moving about and still I don't see a conductor. When the train slows for the fourth time, I say to the women across from me, "Linggries?" She responds, "*Nein.*" I sit. The train stops and goes; the people shift around to refill vacated seats. I go to the bathroom and the train starts to slow. I open the door and say to the first person I see, "Linggries?" "*Nein.*" The train stops and goes. I take a new seat. The train slows, I ask "Linggries?" The response, "*Ya.*" I feel as if I have mastered this new language.

I exit the train by a big step onto a little stool. I walk down the side of the tracks and over a stile. Al waits for me at the fence by the stile. At this meeting, we manage a little kiss. I tell Al he should stop running from country to country, because I will keep following right after him. We tread a path through a small field, to a little train station.

The villages in these mountains have a tradition of each village taking turns having the Friday night entertainment. This Friday, the village of Linggries hosts the big party at our Gasthaus. The people from the other villages have come to Linggries in two big buses that crowd the village's tiny street.

The big room on the ground floor of our Gasthaus is filled with forty or fifty people. We eat dinner family-style, at a long table. When the band starts playing, a big happy German guy asks me to Polka. I keep up pretty well because I learned a few Polka steps from my father when I was a child. When Al and I go upstairs to our room, the *um-pa-pa um-pa-pa* still vibrates the floor. This comfortable happy time remains imbedded in my heart.

After Al got back from Germany, I start working at the PX in the shoe department selling shoes. We settle into a mundane happily married life.

Working in the PX, I make life-long friends. I work with Gerri, the wife to an air force warrant officer, and Fleurie, a French woman of Romanian parentage. Gerri has three children. The oldest is my age. He is living in the States. Her two girls live at home; one is in high school and one in middle school. Fleurie's children, a boy, ten, and a girl, twelve, are delightful. Each morning we must be at work one hour before the PX opens. This hour is used to clean our area and arrange our displays. On the days I work, Fleurie arranges while I do Gerri's hair in the back, where we keep all the shoes. Then Gerri arranges while I do Fleurie's hair. Gerri and Fleurie think this is a real treat, and I don't mind; I don't get a chance to do hair much.

Americans working in the PX must keep their working hours to thirty-four hours per week. This saves the full-time jobs for the French workers. We get paid every other week. So I work thirty-eight hours one week and thirty hours the next. This gives me plenty of time to keep a one-room house. Now, I am always on a day shift. I get upset with Al when he is on night shift, especially if he does not come home first thing in the morning and go to sleep because then, he is sleeping in the evening while I am at home.

Now that we are married and getting dependent pay, Al gets another promotion, and I am working in the PX. Finally, we have some financial breathing room. When I left for France, my mother gave me half of an endowment policy she and my father purchased for their children. I think she held the other half in case my adventure went badly and I needed a ticket home. Understanding all that we went through to get married, she must feel more secure about our ability to live independently. She gives us the rest of the endowment for a downpayment on a car. The car we purchase is a new shiny red Triumph TR4. I earn a reputation at the PX from an incident in this little sports car with a motorcycle gendarme.

Motorcycle gendarmes are acclaimed for always giving a ticket on a traffic stop. I amaze everyone in the PX by getting stopped and not getting a ticket. But I should have gotten a spanking for being a snotty girl.

The PX, the military housing where Gerri lives, and Fleurie's house all lie to the west of the city. This is the direction to go to Versailles from Paris. The course to all these places and back to our apartment makes use of an AutoRoute, which has no posted speed. Just before going into the city the AutoRoute passes through a tunnel. The tunnel has a posted speed limit. I exceed the speed limit through the tunnel and the gendarme pulls me over. He can tell by my license plate that the car belongs to someone in the American military.

He parks his motorcycle behind me and walks up to my window. He says, "*Parlez-vous Francais?*" (Do you speak French?) I say, "No." He says, "*La ou effectue votre travail de pere?*" (Where does your father work?) I say, "*Je ne suis pas ici avec mon pere. Je suis ici avec mon mari!*" (I am not here with my father. I am here with my husband.) The tone and attitude I display while saying this, while trying to appear like an adult must look and sound to him that I am like a spoiled child.

He mumbles something about, "Can't speak French, huh?" and asks to see my papers. I give him my papers. He looks them over and gives me a lecture about going too fast through the tunnel and lets me go.

Another caper that makes me famous with the PX crowd and provides a difficult language ordeal is when the French bloodmobile came to the PX to collect blood. I volunteer to give blood, but first we have to get through the questions like have you ever had hepatitis or malaria. Even the best English speakers have trouble translating these things that don't come up in everyday conversation. We get through the questions and I am young and healthy, so I give a liter of blood. This donation of goodwill outweighs the liter of blood. All the French PX workers think this an admirable thing for an American to do. I didn't know it would be such a big deal, but I delight in doing it.

I have explained my terror when riding in a car through a traffic circle. Now that I wheel the vehicle, I plan my routes to avoid as many of these transit loops as I can. The rule says: Priority to the right for traffic circles. So you must give the right-of-way to everyone on your right, and everyone on your left must yield to you. I have a rule when riding through a traffic circle; I close my eyes. This rule doesn't work well while driving. The circles I do encounter are small and uncrowded yet give me discomfort followed by a feeling of satisfaction when I successfully emerge from the other side. Anyone who has been to Paris knows the biggest traffic circle is situated at the base of the Arc de Triomphe, at the Etoile. Etoile is French for star; all the streets leading into this traffic circle create a star-like pattern. A short block before reaching the Arc is a narrow one-way street that circumnavigates the Etoile, crossing each of the thirteen avenues, which spill onto the Etoile. A traffic light at each avenue makes using the traffic circle the most direct route. The GIs named this ring street "chicken circle," for all of us too chicken to drive out onto the Etoile. Each time I approach the Etoile while driving, I encourage myself to be brave and enter there. But in the end, I always turn onto the chicken circle. >From the Grand e'Armee past Wagrum, Friedland to the Champs Elysees, the ring road's real name is rue de Tilsitt. From Champs Elysees past Victor Hugo and Iena to Grand e'Armee, the rings road's name is rue de Presbourg.

There is one night I would like not to remember because I drank too much. We received an invitation to a wedding reception for the niece of a colonel. I don't know anything about this wedding, how it was done, or even why we are invited. I forgot about the reception and when Al picks me up after work, we didn't have time to go back home for me to change. I went to the reception in my wool skirt, cotton blouse, and penny loafers. At the reception women in the most beautiful cocktail dresses I have ever seen surround me. I can do nothing about the dumb clothes I wear, so I get drunk.

Sgt. Blessim, the guy with the little car at the airport upon my arrival in Paris, is there with a French woman who speaks no English. Sgt. Blessim dates a lot of women who do not speak English. I do not know where he meets them, and I don't think he speaks French that well. After getting drunk I talk to this French woman all evening. She is very nice, and I talk to her in French. We joke, we laugh, and she says she understands me just fine. Sober, I have no idea how I did it. But I remember the gist of our conversation. A warrant officer who started working at the BlockHouse a couple of months before this has heard from the guys that Al is married to an American girl. I have never met him, so at this party, he introduces himself to me. I am so mean. He talks to me in English and I will only answer him in French. He keeps saying, "You are American right?" And each time I answer, "*Oui*." The poor guy, he goes back to the BlockHouse the next day and tells all the guys, he met Al's wife and she is French. My new French friend thought my teasing this guy this way was very funny.

Al told me one time that I woke him by talking in my sleep. I was saying, "*Je ne comprends pas*" (I don't understand).

On our days off in the summer we enjoy going to the swimming pools that are on barges tethered in the river. There are two of them close to metro stop Assemblee Nationale.

A swimming pool barge is really a clever thing when you need to insert something that large into an old crowded city. It is anchored in the river and a plank extends to the *Quai* (embankment). You enter by the plank, pay at the pay window, go down the stairs where there are locker rooms and a snack counter, and a big plank deck for sunbathing surrounds the pool. These pools are no longer there. We read years ago that one of them burned.

Other days off we like to go to the big department stores Printemps and Galleries Lafayette to look around. Looking is all we can afford to do. Our favorite store for buying things like cards and a few tools is the Prisunic on the Champs Elysees. Prisunic is more like a Woolworth's. Downstairs in the Prisunic now there is a supermarket, but when we lived there this area held hardware. I did buy a bikini at Printemps. I had to be properly adorned when we went to the swimming pool.

My biggest disappointment was the Bastille Day Parade. Raised in the United States, I know about parades. On Thanksgiving I watched the Macy's Parade, and on New Year's Day I watched the Rose Bowl Parade on TV. I have seen magnificent flowered floats and fabulous character balloons. Now, I am in Paris. Paris, the capital of the world of style, I must be about to see the most wonderful parade imaginable. We take the metro to the Franklin D. Roosevelt stop. I have never been in such a crowd. We struggle up the Champs Elysees and stand five people deep to try and get a view. Jet fighter planes fly over. The crowd sounds an *aha*. Tanks begin to roll by. Big guns wheel past. French soldiers march the course. It starts to sink in. This is not going to be a parade of beautiful flowers and giant balloons. I did get a peek and a picture of General De Gaulle; I guess that is as good as a rose queen.

We went to dinner at the home of Janine's parents the second Thanksgiving. Dinner was in the evening because this is a regular workday for Janine's dad and school day for Janine's younger sister. This was the only time I met Janine's dad. He is a very charming man, and her mother is delightful. We have a wonderful time and a good dinner.

Our second Christmas Al is working afternoon shift and arrives home about midnight, Christmas Eve. We talk about opening our presents then, but I like the tradition of opening presents on Christmas morning. We go to bed but when we can't sleep, we agree that technically, it is Christmas morning. We get up to open the presents. I have to put in my contact lenses and I lose one down the drain. Al gets a wrench from the car, takes the drain apart, and retrieves my lens. This is the best Christmas present! I cannot function without my lenses, and I have no glasses.

Al and I heard about romantic dinners on a boat called Bateaux Mouches traveling down the Seine. I want to go there for our first anniversary. The boat doesn't run in the wintertime so instead, we go to the Lido. The Lido is a prime nightclub with a fabulous show located on the Champs Elysees. Years later, the Lido moved back into a shopping area off the Champs Elysees. Nowadays it is just not the high profile place it was in 1965. I bought a black lace dress at the PX and we really have a lovely evening. My assessment of the evening: a perfect anniversary. Al said the fish course at dinner made him sick.

In 1989 we visit Paris in May to celebrate our twenty-fifth anniversary. We finally have dinner on the Bateaux Mouches. The dinner and the ride down the Seine are outstandingly romantic. The tables are arranged so each couple sits side by side and faces the front of the boat. This cozy arrangement creates a feeling of isolation from the rest of the passengers. The couple seated in front of us is young, and the girl has very long, fine blond hair hanging down her back. Toward the end of the evening her date embraces her with a passionate kiss. As they embrace, her head comes toward our table until her hair reaches our candle. The fire flares quickly and Al begins to smack her head to put out the flames. She struggles because her head is being walloped. Her date mistakes her action for passion, and pushes her further back. She finally fights out of his arms and turns to face us. The fire is now in her eyes. She has no idea why her head was whacked. We show them the candle and the plight she encountered. By then the smell of burning hair tells the story without words or pantomime.

Again, a perfect anniversary. I am happy we did the Lido on our first anniversary and saved the Bateaux Mouches for twenty-four years later; everything turned out for the best.

The time to return to the States came all too soon. Al thought about reenlisting so we could stay longer. It is now spring 1965, and a problem developing in a little country called Viet Nam makes Al decide against re-enlistment. After re-enlistment, the army can send him wherever they wish. Horace re-enlisted and he stayed in Paris until DeGaulle had all foreign military removed in 1967. Then he and Christina finished his tour in Berlin. This would have been perfect for us, but Al didn't want to take a chance of being sent to Viet Nam. The State Department people told Al he could have a job with them after the army. Traveling the world sounded like fun, but the glamour would probably wear off after the first six moves.

Enlisted GIs get one hundred pounds of whole baggage that the army will ship home for them. Amey gets his orders to return the same time Al gets his orders. They are both returning to Denver. Amey is so very kind; he gives us his allotment of whole baggage. Two wooden boxes are delivered to our apartment. They are slightly longer and somewhat skinnier than coffins. They sit in the middle of the floor for several days while I pack them.

As we prepare to leave France, we turn over our apartment to some other GIs so they don't have to pay an agent fee. Al is on the ship on his way home. I am staying with Gerri and her family. Gerri and I visit Fleurie at her home one evening. We are watching TV at Fleurie's and I am translating for Gerri. Fleurie compliments me on my good rendition. Maybe now if I were to ask someone the time, I could understand the answer.

Modest Americans have always been fascinated and revolted by the French public restrooms. The *pissoir* was conveniently located on busy streets while I lived there. There was a circular partition of drab green metal about six feet tall and open on the bottom about a foot and a half. Not a closed circle. When you enter there was a little low birdbath like fountain into which a standing man could relieve himself. I was told the partition was added in the mid-twentieth century. That would be a decade or so before I arrived. These conveniences served well, but as a woman, I am happy when I find the new closet into which anyone can enter, even a woman, with the proper coinage. These are called *sanesettes payantes*. My entire stay I had heard stories of restrooms that were floor drains with painted footprints showing the place one should stand. I had never encountered one of these until I was on my way to the airport to return to the States. To close this perfect circle of exciting, enchanting, and exasperating adventures, I ask Sgt. Blessim to drive me to the airport on the day of my departure. He picked me up at Gerri's house and had with him a new recruit, so again I was stuffed into this small car. I did not sit on the recruit's lap. We squeezed in three across, and I gave up room for the floor shift. Halfway to the airport, all three of us needed a restroom. We stopped at a café and were directed down the stairs. I went to the women's room and found the infamous footprints. I think this startles Americans because you are looking for a toilet and find what looks more like a shower. I took one look and decided I was not prepared to hold up my skirt and try to keep my feet and legs from getting splashed. If I were to miss and splash myself, I would be living in that condition for many hours as I traveled to New York. So I said *huh* to my discovery and returned to the car. Once back on the road headed for the airport, I took a peek at Sgt. Blessim's and the recruit's shoes and saw their splashes. I have since this time had the pleasure of using this kind of convenience. There are times when you must go. Nowadays on the AutoRoutes, this is the only kind of restroom you will find. They are easy to keep clean.

The actual time we spent living in Paris is very short compared to the amount of influence living in Paris has made on our lives. To this day when the Arc de Triomphe appears on the TV or movie screen my heart leaps with longing. Paris will always feel like home.

Returning to the States generates new adjustments. We stayed in a motel on Long Island waiting for the car to be shipped back. The women cleaning the motel rooms speak to me and I understand everything they say, even with their Queens accent. Oh, English. The workers in this country speak English. After spending so much time adrift, understanding little of what was happening around me, a simple chat or greeting is unexpected. When our car arrives we start our drive cross-country in a bitter cold snowstorm for all of Pennsylvania and Ohio. In Cleveland we stop to visit Ray and meet the lucky girl. Ray returned to Cleveland a couple of months earlier and will be married in June.

In Iowa we stop in Council Bluffs where Al was born. We have dinner in Council Bluffs at Al's family's favorite restaurant. Without thinking, we order a bottle of wine. The waiter immediately asks to see our IDs. We both laugh, but the waiter, a middle-aged American, didn't find any humor in it. Al is twenty-one, but I am still a couple of months short of that magic age. The waiter brought the wine to Al and stood by Al through dinner to be sure I didn't imbibe.

Al took a business trip which gave him a day in Paris in 1976. On a survey of all our old haunts, he found the BlockHouse with a big hole blown in the sidewalk. By the time we returned as a family in 1982 we found a new modern building standing in place of the BlockHouse. This trip, after eighteen years of longing to return, was pleasing because of the things that had not changed. Showing our daughter all our favorite places and telling her all our fun stories made this family vacation a delight. So after several trips over another eighteen years I have learned to tolerate the changes in Paris, along with the loss of my youth.

My most recent trip to Paris after I had started to write this account of my plight was to the Prefecture de Police. I walked completely around the building; it seems so much smaller. I am viewing it on a sunny Sunday in mid-March, not a gloomy Friday in January. I see now it is so close to Notre Dame and surrounded by tourists. Yet, I still see in my mind's eye high, dark walls oppressing me. I locate the metro stop on each side of the river and still cannot find the scary picture residing in my head. Closer investigation inside the metro stop, in one of Paris' oldest metro stops, reveals a stairway to nowhere. It has been closed off. The trip around the building exposes the entrance to the underground parking. The large, newly tiled walkway at street level now covers my canyon of fear.

I believe the Paris experience to be life-altering, no matter what age you are when you are there, and no matter what age she is when you are first introduced. I feel privileged to have known her when tourists were few, and to visit her now with her arms and her boulevards opened so the world can stroll the Champs Elysees.

After all these years, Al and I seem to have a special bond because **"We will always have Paris."**